THE PARENT'S GUIDE TO
CAMPING WITH CHILDREN

THE PARENT'S GUIDE TO

CAMPING *With* CHILDREN

Roger and Kimberley Woodson

BETTERWAY BOOKS

CINCINNATI, OHIO

The Parent's Guide to Camping With Children. Copyright © 1995 by Roger and Kimberley Woodson. Printed and bound in the United States of America. All rights reserved. No part of this book may be reproduced in any form or by any electronic or mechanical means including information storage and retrieval systems without permission in writing from the publisher, except by a reviewer, who may quote brief passages in a review. Published by Betterway Books, an imprint of F&W Publications, Inc., 1507 Dana Avenue, Cincinnati, Ohio 45207. 1-800-289-0963. First edition.

99 98 97 96 95   5 4 3 2 1

Library of Congress Cataloging-in-Publication Data

Woodson, R. Dodge (Roger Dodge).
  The parent's guide to camping with children / Roger and Kimberley Woodson.
    p.   cm.
  Includes index.
  ISBN 1-55870-352-7
  1. Camping. 2. Camping—Equipment and supplies. 3. Family recreation.
  I. Woodson, Kimberley. II. Title. III. Title: Camping with children.
GV191.7.W66 1995
796.54—dc20   94-35285
                                                           CIP

Edited by David G. Tompkins
Cover and interior design by Sandy Conopeotis
Cover photos by Superstock

This book is dedicated to our wonderful daughter, Afton.

Roger Woodson

Roger Woodson is the author of dozens of books and magazine articles. In addition to his writing, he owns several businesses in the fields of real estate, plumbing, general contracting, and training and development. He and his wife, Kimberley, have a daughter, Afton, and a second child due in the coming months.

Roger started camping in his backyard some thirty years ago. His love of animals, nature, and the outdoors acted as a catalyst for his camping experiences. As an avid wildlife and nature photographer, Roger backpacked and camped for much of his early life, and has always enjoyed playing the role of a "Mountain Man."

When Afton was born, Roger and Kimberley took a hiatus of several years from camping. Though afraid to take their baby into the woods, they bought a travel trailer and rekindled their interests in camping, this time with a child. Roger believes the experience, while very different, is more rewarding and enjoyable when the world is seen through the eyes of a youngster.

Roger sold the travel trailer and reverted to tent camping a few years ago. When the new baby arrives, there will be little time lost from camping. The experience he has gained as a father has proven to him that camping with a young child is not only possible, but can be a lot of fun.

Kimberley Woodson

Kimberley Woodson has worked with Roger on several books providing resource information. She is the Director of Administration for a national health care organization and specializes in human resources, corporate training and computer applications. Kimberley has also done volunteer work with children for numerous civic groups since 1970.

Kimberley has been camping since she was a child. She has been from Maine to California with her parents and two brothers. Many of her recommendations come from activities she first enjoyed as a youngster, which are now an integral part of camping with her own family. She feels that if parents provide the opportunity for children to experience nature through their senses and instinctive curiosity, they will gain a lasting appreciation for and understanding of their world.

Kimberley and her family value the quality time they spend camping in the peaceful woods and along the stunning coast of Maine. She feels there is no toy you can buy a child which will be treasured as dearly as those gifts provided by nature. The joys of seeing a bald eagle soar over your head, discovering a tidal pool teeming with tiny sea creatures, or snuggling together around a crackling fire toasting marshmallows cannot be duplicated on TV or sold in a department store.

Kimberley has camped in a lean-to, tent, pop-up trailer, and travel trailer. No matter what level of accommodation is used, she feels that camping with children is the most rewarding way to experience nature: You rediscover the world through their eyes.

Roger, Kimberley and Afton live in Bowdoinham, Maine.

INTRODUCTION

Do you like to go camping? Has your camping activity slowed down since having a child? If so, this book is for you. Before we became parents, we went camping frequently. After having our first child, camping trips were no longer a part of our routine plans. At first, we were willing to sacrifice our love of the outdoors and camping as a trade-off for having had a wonderful daughter. In time, the old desire to get back into the woods with a tent and a sleeping bag became stronger and stronger. The problem was that we were afraid to take our daughter, Afton, camping in the wilds of Maine.

After languishing for some time, we summoned up the courage to strike out on a camping trip with our youngster. The first trip was tense and not very enjoyable. It was nothing like our camping trips used to be. In time, however, we adapted to traveling and camping with a young child. Not only did we adapt, but we found the experience to be fulfilling beyond our expectations.

Camping with kids is very different from taking off with a group of adults for a weekend in the wilderness, but the difference can be very pleasing. This book will share with you the experience we have gained from camping with a child.

You are going to find out what modifications will be needed to your list of camping gear. Our tips on how to travel with a young child will make getting to camp a lot more fun. There is a host of suggestions waiting for you in the following pages. We hope that you will not make the mistake that we did when we decided not to go camping because we had brought a child into the world.

It would not be fair to tell you that camping with children is simple, easy, or always enjoyable. The fact is, if you don't know how to go about it, camping with kids can be more trouble than it is worth. This book will help you avoid the problems associated with camping with your children, and more importantly, it will guide you to ways of enjoying life like you never have before.

Chapter One

THE BENEFITS OF FAMILY CAMPING

It's Friday afternoon, and as you sit in your office, listening to the clamor of office machines and the echoing of ringing telephones, you wish you could get away from it all. All you want is to escape the noise, the deadlines, the phones and the responsibilities, just to live life for a few days. You remember the days before the kids, the dog, the soccer games, and the ballet recitals. That was when you and your spouse would run off to the woods for weekends to relax in the wilderness.

What's stopping you from your wilderness retreats now? Pack up the kids, the dog, the radio headphones, the hand-held video games, and the nearly 200 pounds of camping gear, and you're on your way to a weekend of peace and quiet. Somehow it's just not the same as it used to be, is it?

The prospect of kids constantly asking "Are we there yet?" and "How much farther is it?" or complaining "I'm bored" is not conducive to camping enjoyment. Having children screaming like banshees in the bushes or whining inside the tent eliminates camping from the list of fun things to do for many parents. They don't realize that as with everything in life, there is a right way to take a family excursion and a wrong way. Kids do not have to be a camping curse you dread. Done correctly, camping with your children can be one of the most enriching, rewarding experiences you share as a family.

Many of our fondest childhood memories are of camping, and those positive experiences encouraged us to continue a family tradition of enjoying nature as a family. We did take a brief hiatus when our daughter was born, but we soon got back into camping, and it has been great!

Have you ever looked at the world through the eyes of your children? When your daughter ran into the kitchen with a ladybug or your son pulled you outside to marvel at a rainbow the sprinkler was making, perhaps you saw these things in a new way. Wonderful experiences such as these are multiplied a hundred times when camping. Your children will see things you might never notice, hear things you ignore, and catch aromas on the breeze that you miss. Basically, your kids will discover the world around them and gladly and proudly share every aspect of those treasures with you.

EDUCATIONAL VALUE

The educational value of camping cannot be ignored. No matter how old your children are, they can always learn something new on a camping expedition. The possibilities are endless. You can teach your child that everything in life has its own role and importance, such as acorns sprouting new trees and earthworms aerating the soil.

A walk along a stream will often reveal the tracks of animals. By observing these tracks, children can piece together the puzzle of what the animal was doing. While this will seem like a game to your kids, it will be teaching them to use deductive reasoning. Life is a learning experience and so is camping.

When we camped as a couple, we sought the wilderness as a refuge from our busy adult lives. We spent a lot of time just reading, or passively wandering through the woods. Camping takes on a much more interactive shape when children are involved. It becomes a learning experience filled with touching, feeling, squeals of excitement, whispers of anticipation, and an abundance of smiles. You behold an independence and enthusiasm in your children which is often obscured by daily routines. Your children see you as a teacher, a guide, the wise woodsperson, the firemaker, and a hero. Your family gains new insight and respect, not only for nature but for each other as well. These are not possibilities or probabilities, these are the inherent by-products of putting adults, children and Mother Nature in the same space together, under the proper conditions.

Ah, but what if it rains on those conditions? What if Suzy is afraid of the dark or Billy has a brush with poison ivy? Maybe you should go to the beach or the amusement park and spend the night in a hotel instead. But by the time you pay for a hotel room, food, tickets, parking and miscellaneous fees, the average family of four can easily spend over $300 for a single getaway weekend. This type of expenditure adds up quickly, and can put a serious dent in most anyone's budget. What's a better option? Camping.

A LOW-BUDGET VACATION ALTERNATIVE

When you are rearing your children, money can be difficult to manage. It seems that no matter how fast your income rolls in, it rolls out even faster. With so many mandatory financial obligations like clothes, food, utilities, car payments and house payments, it can be hard to find ways to enjoy quality time with your family without breaking your budget. Camping gives you the opportunity to explore your family and your world, without much cash.

Getting the gear necessary to go camping isn't a big financial burden. For that matter, you can opt for the rental plan and have no acquisition costs. There are companies that rent pop-up trailers, tag-along trailers, and motorhomes.

Many different styles of camping are available to you. For one family a lean-to and a few blankets will be all that is needed to get outside and live the outdoors life. Another family might prefer the creature comforts found in travel trailers and motorhomes. The difference in cost for these varying types of camping escalates based on the number and kind of amenities you choose. While lean-to campers can get into camping for less than $50, those who buy a motorhome could easily invest $50,000.

Camping is not cost-prohibitive. For a onetime investment in basic supplies, you and your family can enjoy countless hours of camping. Most people choose to invest more money, but the choice is yours. If you camped before you had children, you will be pleasantly surprised at how little new equipment you need to acquire.

As for the costs of routine camping, you can get by on nearly nothing. With the abundance of public camping areas available, you can find a site that suits your budget. It is often possible to camp free in parks and National Forests. If you prefer a more civilized site, you can rent space in a campground for less than ten dollars per night. Think about it: where else can a family of four spend the night for less than ten dollars?

COOKING OUT

Almost everyone enjoys cooking out from time to time, but so often it is confined to the backyard grill. However, when you are camping, cooking out takes on a whole new meaning. Instead of spraying starter fluid on charcoal, you gather tinder, kindling and wood. With the right combination of natural materials, there is no need for squirting volatile fluids on your outdoor heat source.

Of course, there can be a little extra work involved with campfire cookery, but the work is fun. Instead of walking out and lifting the top off your grill, you and your children may have to collect rocks to build your fireplace. Designing and building your own fire ring can be fun. The search for firewood is equally as entertaining, especially when you make it a contest to see who can find the most wood. Your tiniest tykes can help by gathering dry leaves and twigs to start the fire.

Once the fireplace is ready and filled with good, natural fire materials, you are ready to light the fire. As the fire begins to burn, your nose will experience the wonderful aroma of wild wood smoke. There is something about the taste of food cooked on an open fire that is beyond compare. You don't get this type of pleasure with a backyard barbecue.

After your meal is prepared, you can recline against a tree and enjoy the smells and tastes of eating in the wild. Instead of watching the same old boring television shows while you eat, you can stare into the flickering flames and lose yourself in imagination. You will begin to feel like a kid again.

HEALTH BENEFITS

There are many health benefits related to camping; just getting out into the fresh air is enough for most people, but there is much more. You can hike for hours. We all know that walking is a solid form of exercise, and what better way is there to get your work-out than walking nature's trails? Your kids will keep you plenty active, too, running through the trees, swimming in the lake, and bending, kneeling and reaching to see and feel everything around you. These are all great exercise.

RECREATIONAL OPPORTUNITIES

Camping offers endless hours of fun for kids and grown-ups alike. Whether it is collecting acorns, floating leaves down a stream in a mock boat race, or toasting marshmallows over an open fire, fun can be found in every aspect of the outdoor experience. The recreational opportunities that go hand in hand with camping are mind-boggling.

If you elect to stay in organized campgrounds, you are likely to find swimming pools, playgrounds, recreational centers, tennis, volleyball and basketball courts, and more.

When you choose to take a less formal approach to camping, you will have the world at your feet: there will be fishing, hunting, hiking, bird watching, swimming, wading, sketching, photography, and as many forms of crafts and scientific discoveries as you and your children can absorb.

QUALITY TIME

Quality family time is hard to come by these days. In our fast-paced daily life, we have lost something of great value: family time. When was the last time you and your family had breakfast together? How long has it been since you engaged in conversation with your whole family for more than fifteen minutes? Can you remember the last time you spent an evening without turning on the radio or television? With all the modern technology and business focus of the present, we have forgotten what families of the past had.

The families that kept the home fires burning in the old farmhouse didn't have television and talking spaceships. There were no mechanical toys that told bedtime stories to the children. Families relied on each other for entertainment. In getting away from the simple forms of family activity, people are losing touch with each other.

Camping resuscitates many of the pastimes enjoyed by our ancestors. You can sit around the glowing embers and tell stories. Whittling a stick can provide more pleasure than flipping through channels with the remote control. An old-fashioned card game will allow time to talk and enjoy the moment. When an owl hoots and startles you, you can sense the need you have for each other.

While there is nothing wrong with keeping up with our ever-changing future, there is also nothing wrong with stepping back in time to a simpler lifestyle. Camping is an ideal vehicle for these trips back to times almost forgotten. Many important lessons can be taught in the outdoor classroom of the campsite.

CAMPING REWARDS

The rewards of camping are many, and the drawbacks are few. If you are looking for an inexpensive way to enjoy time with your family, camping is hard to beat. In purchasing this book, you have taken the first step toward procuring economical, enjoyable family vacations. We will share generations of family camping tips and secrets with you in order to help you avoid or resolve almost every camping dilemma. With proper planning and help from everyone in the family, you will experience camping and each other in a whole new and exciting light.

Chapter Two

CAMPING IN THE BACKYARD

Do you remember the last time you were in unfamiliar surroundings or thrust into uncomfortable circumstances? Can you remember having feelings of apprehension, anxiety, self-doubt or fear? Now, think about the last time you were required to learn and master a new job skill. Perhaps it was using the latest version of a computer software program or just adapting to a recent change in company procedure. On the personal side, maybe you were only attempting to master a new tennis or golf stroke. Did you jump into the process without any sense of direction, or did you slowly proceed, step by step, until you were comfortable with the procedure?

Most people learn new things in stages. They develop skills by progressing from the initial orientation phase to the repetitious, hands-on, practice-makes-perfect level. Gradually their understanding and appreciation for a new circumstance or technique evolves. In order to advance within a process, people must also overcome their inherent fears and apprehensions of the unknown and of failing.

These concepts and risks are familiar to many adults, but foreign and intimidating to most children. All too often parents forget how difficult the learning process can be. They thrust their children into uncomfortable situations and set the stage for rebellion, anger or fear, and sometimes for all of them at once.

Imagine toting children into the woods, zipping them into a cold sleeping bag on hard ground, and telling them to go to sleep to the sounds of hooting owls and rasping bugs. What may feel like peaceful, relaxing surroundings to you can seem like a nightmare to an unprepared child. Children learn about the world not by drawing on adult logic, but rather by feeling and interacting with their surroundings. They experience the world tactilely. Their senses are one of the few things in the world children can control. This is why they ask questions, questions that can seem strange and unimportant to busy parents.

What kinds of questions are kids likely to ask? They may ask what a bear smells like, or what a bat sounds like. A curious child may very well want to know how cold it has to be to freeze a person. This type of questioning is not stupid or childish. The questions are fair, and in many ways responsible. The parent who cannot answer such questions is at a disadvantage; you should become as knowledgeable as possible.

PREPARATION FOR THE UNFAMILIAR

Before you load up the family car for several days of camping in an unknown place, you should take some time to prepare your children for the trip. This preparation can take place in your own backyard, or even in your living room.

Children believe that if they can see it, smell it, hear it, feel it, or taste it, they can satisfy their curiosity or overcome their fear. As a parent, you can remove most of the fear and frustration a child may experience from a first camping trip before you ever leave home. This not only helps the child, it will make your life much easier when you are afield.

It is your job to prepare your children to experience camping as a positive adventure, not as a frightening, hostile battle with the unknown. To do this, you must remember two key procedures: keep your approach interesting and interactive. Let's look at some methods which have worked for us, and for other camping parents.

What Kind of Animals Live in the Woods?

One of our daughter's first questions about camping was what kinds of animals live in the woods. Residing in Maine, we told her she could expect to find signs of rabbits, squirrels, deer, moose, porcupines, raccoons, skunks, and many other types of wildlife, even eagles. That was all Afton needed to hear. She made up her mind right then and there that she was not going to spend the night in a tent. The idea of sleeping at ground level, in a nylon tent, was not appealing to her. Even though Afton was very young, she had seen moose up close and knew how big they can get. Waiting in a flimsy tent to be trampled by a moose, sprayed by a skunk, or poked by a porcupine was not Afton's idea of fun.

We were glad that we had the foresight to omit coyotes and bears from the list, but needless to say, we had to do some quick thinking to find a way of dispelling her concerns. We therefore took the time to educate Afton on the subject of wild animals.

Many animals can pose a threat to people without any intent of malice. Afton's concern of being run over by a moose was not so farfetched. Moose don't have great eyesight, and if a big bull was being chased by Maine's legendary black flies, it is entirely possible he might pay little attention to a tiny tent in his path. While this type of situation is highly unlikely, it is possible.

Our daughter has a mind that can dissect the most tightly woven parental con job. To tell Afton that a moose couldn't trample our tent would have been a big mistake. She would have known it was possible, and such an answer to her question would have diminished her trust and confidence in the two of us.

So what did we do? We talked with Afton about what each of the animals she might encounter was like. She asked some very intelligent questions, like where do porcupines sleep? I knew I had seen them sleeping in trees, but to be sure, we went to the library in search of answers. We learned, to Afton's relief, that porcupines prefer sleeping in trees to crashing through tents and bunking in with little girls.

Afton found a delightful book, *The Adventures of Maynard . . . a Maine Moose*, by Maine author Marybeth Baker. It is the story of a big, clumsy, yet very gentle moose and his forest friends. Characters like chattering Rebecca Raccoon, graceful Eldon Eagle, timid Dora Deer, wise Justin Bear, and odd-looking Pearl Porcupine came together to illustrate the wonders of nature in Maine. By the time we had finished at the library, Afton could hardly wait to go home and start her list of animal tracks to look for.

Other Fears

Other children may be more concerned with issues such as darkness, noises, or simply sleeping in a new place. We've had friends tell us their children had just as difficult a time sleeping in a hotel as in a tent. This makes plenty of sense, since the basic elements of displacement and adapting to new circumstances exist whether you are in a hotel, motorhome or tent.

Children who have no problem sleeping at home will unexpectedly ask for a night-light or bedtime story when they go camping. Other children may seem concerned that the tent will collapse or that they will run out of drinking water.

No amount of assurance on your part can erase these fears completely. Sometimes, the easiest way to acclimate your apprehensive youngsters to a new situation is to have a test run. Consider an overnight camp-out in your backyard. In preparation for backyard camping, talk with your children to find out what concerns they may have. You will be astonished by the number of thoughts children have that don't occur to adults.

Where will we go potty? That is one of the first questions your kids may have. What will we do if the wind blows our tent over? How will we cook dinner? What will we do with our trash? Suppose we get caught in a thunderstorm? We will help you answer these questions and others in the following chapters of this book.

It's all right to admit to your children that you haven't worked out every possible scenario. Ask them for their ideas and potential solutions. It is entirely possible your children will have some strong input on how to solve a problem. You can encourage your children to seek out solutions by using your adult logic to spark their sensory responses. If your daughter is concerned about the dark, suggest that she go through the house and look for items that can be taken on camping trips as light sources. She may return with everything from flashlights to glow-in-the-dark stickers. Take these along on your field trip and let your daughter pick which item provides her with the security she requires. Your children will, with your help, learn to answer their own questions.

THE GREAT LIVING-ROOM WILDERNESS

Have you ever thought of exploring the great living-room wilderness? One urban couple we know planned a camp-out in the living room of their apartment. They wanted to closely simulate the outdoors and to think of something for dinner that wouldn't require a fire or stove. Their toddler recommended cheese sandwiches, because they were full of energy, did not need to be cooked, and wouldn't stick in her mouth and make her thirsty, like peanut butter sandwiches might. They all agreed to wash their plates in the stream (the bathtub) so they wouldn't have a lot of paper plates and trash to take home (into the kitchen) after their trip.

One of the couple's older children considered the problem of garbage for his impending trial trip. He prepared paper bags labeled "Food Cans," "Paper," "Bottles and Cans $." He announced that his family would need to protect the "wilderness" from pollution while they were camping. He was to be awarded the bottle and can deposit money the next day in return for his conscientious solution.

This family went on their home-based camping trip and had a great time. The next weekend, the family went to the woods for real, and they had an even better time. The mock camping trip at home allowed the family to work out the minor glitches that may have ruined an on-location camping trip. You can use this same type of trial run to work the bugs out of your camping plans.

The Dry-Run Approach

The dry-run approach is an excellent way to reacquaint yourself with your camping gear and to get your children interested in the camping process.

During these introductory camping expeditions, be sure to include your children in all aspects of the packing and preparation for the make-believe trip. You can use the checklists in chapter three for your trial run. Many of these items can be gathered by your children. If your child is too young to read a list, consider cutting pictures of the required items out of a magazine and letting your youngster glue them into a camping book.

Once you reach your intended destination, be it the backyard, the living room, or an actual campground, invite your children to help prepare the campsite. They can clear the area for the tent or trailer, gather wood and kindling (for a make-believe fire if necessary), and hold poles or tent stakes while you erect your shelter for the night. Take the time to explain how the tension of the tent ropes against the frame keeps the tent from collapsing, and ask your children to strum the ropes to check for slack.

A dry run is an ideal opportunity to work through some of the basic fears your children may have about going into the woods. It is also a great chance to remember, or learn, how to set up your tent and other camping equipment. Let's take a few moments to do a quick rundown of how a mock camping trip might go.

The Packing Phase

The packing phase can be a real problem. As family cars have gotten smaller, it is more difficult than ever to get all the necessities loaded and leave room for passengers and pets. Big kids will want to take bikes, boom boxes, and such. Smaller children may want to take along their favorite, nearly life-size, stuffed animals. If you have really young children, there may be a need for playpens, portable cribs, and other baby-related gear.

If you don't take some control over what your children take on camping trips, you may need a 40-foot trailer to haul it all. While you can't give them carte blanche, you must allow children, especially youngsters, to take a few personal and favorite items for security and comfort. It is much better to work out the details of what will, and will not, be going camping well ahead of an actual field trip. By staging a mock trip, you can identify all the mandatory items and cull the crop to a manageable size. The next chapter will give you all the help you need in this stage of your camping development.

Simulated Travel Time

Simulated travel time is not an essential element of a mock trip, but it may help to take the edge off of a real trip. If nothing else, you should consider what types of toys and games you and your children will use to reduce the boredom of traveling. Time on the road can be a deterrent to camping with kids, but it doesn't have to be.

Making Camp

Chapter six gives you the facts on making camp for real, but let's look at how you can improvise in your backyard or living room. If you are going to simulate your camping trip in the backyard, you can follow the instructions in chapter six. If, however, you live in an apartment or townhouse, you may not have enough ground to pitch a tent on. If that's the case, you can go through the motions in your own living room.

Even if your tent has a floor in it, and most modern tents do, you should put a ground cover under the tent. The ground cover, usually a tarp, protects the tent floor from ground moisture and punctures. If your kids are large enough to walk, they can help with the laying of the ground cover.

Some tents, usually umbrella tents, can be set up without the use of tent stakes. This is not normally a good idea in the wild, but it is great in the home. If your tent requires the use of tent stakes, you can use rocks, books, or even furniture in place of stakes. As long as the items are heavy enough to keep tension on the tent ropes, you shouldn't have any problem.

A fireplace can be built out of rocks, books, pillows, or any other simulated material. The kids can collect the fireplace materials, just as they would on a real camp-out, if they are old enough. Obviously, you should not build an open fire in your home, unless you have an approved, permanent fireplace. If you are fortunate enough to own a home with a real fireplace, building a fire is a wonderful idea; you can even roast marshmallows or hot dogs. We like to do this from time to time, just for the fun of it.

Getting Settled In

Getting settled in is one of the most important aspects of your first camping trip with your children. This is when you make your campsite a home away from home, and it is also the time when some youngsters will change their attitudes about being in the great outdoors.

If you put yourself in your child's place, a light in the tent at night can create some frightening shadows. This may not seem like a big deal to you, but a child's imagination can create some serious problems. There are numerous situations that may arise in a real camping situation to scare the daylights out of your children. Chapter twelve is going to show you how to make it through the night on real camping trips, but let us give you some primer advice now.

Eliminating Your Children's Fears

Eliminating preexisting fears is one of the most beneficial tactics you as a parent can take in preparing a child for a real camping trip. As you learned earlier, our daughter was afraid of forest animals. Not all children are alike, and many of them will have different kinds of fears. For example, another fear Afton used to have was that of how her pets would survive while we were away. Once she knew we had made arrangements to have her pets taken care of, she was fine. It doesn't always take a masters degree in psychology or years of experience as a parent to remove a child's fear. In fact, there are often quick, easy solutions to what seem like very serious concerns.

Children may be frightened by the shadows cast on the inside of a tent. Your mock trip can remove these fears. You can even make a game out of having a shadow puppet show to eliminate fear.

You may find in your mock trip that going to the bathroom is a problem for your child. Using portable toilet facilities is not the same as going to the bathroom in your home. By conducting a test run, you can determine what your needs will be for privacy and comfort.

Sleeping inside a sleeping bag can be a scary experience for a child. Some people don't like to feel confined when sleeping. This may rule out the use of mummy-style sleeping bags. This is something you can find out in the comfort and control of your own home.

Wilderness sounds account for much of the fear children harbor in real camping. Unless you live on a farm, you may have trouble allowing your child to experience these sounds before going afield. The croaking of a bullfrog can strike fear into a kid's heart, and the screech of an owl can make getting to sleep all but impossible.

People living in cities may never have seen cows, let alone a deer, moose or bear. We have seen parents at zoos and wildlife parks mistake pheasants for wild turkeys and foxes for coyotes. How can you begin to break the ice on animal sounds if you live in an urban environment? Audio and video tapes can go a long way in preparing your child for animal sounds and behavior. Audio tapes that depict cascading brooks, the sounds of loons, and other outdoor sounds are great primers. Videos that show wildlife habits are also ideal ways to introduce your children to the appearance, habits, actions and sounds of nature's creatures. These tapes are frequently available at music stores, video rental stores, bookstores, sporting goods stores and novelty stores.

Parental Concerns

There is more than just your child's fears to overcome. You must overcome your own fears. Taking your child into strange surroundings can be a stressful experience for responsible parents. There are many viable fears you may feel, and we will address those issues throughout the book. Kimberley and I both had our own reservations about taking Afton into the wilderness of northern Maine.

Prior to becoming parents, we were always tent campers. In fact, before I met Kimberley, I used to backpack extensively and rarely used a tent. I have slept in the proximity of bears, coyotes, porcupines, bobcats, moose, skunks, and even cougars, without incident. Certainly, these occasions could have been considered risky, and I wouldn't recommend taking your child into a dangerous situation. However, upon reviewing crime statistics, you may find your children are much safer in the wilderness than they are in the city.

If you or your child are not comfortable with sleeping in a tent, there are still many camping options available to you. As a matter of fact, we could not bring ourselves to take Afton camping in a tent in the Maine wilderness. When we decided to get back into camping, we bought a small travel trailer. The trailer provided many advantages over tent camping. These advantages are described in chapter fifteen.

After working through our fears, tent camping is again our current mode of camping. Afton and Kimberley were never against tent camping, but being a protective father, I was. As an adult, I have taken all kinds of risks and enjoyed the outdoors to the fullest. But when it came to putting my daughter in any type of possible danger, I couldn't do it.

If you fail to address your own fears, you may be doing an injustice to your child. Children learn from their parents. If you provide too much protection for your child, you may be doing more harm than good. I believe you must allow children to learn on their own, under controlled circumstances. Certainly, you wouldn't allow your child to play with a rattlesnake to find out that rattlers can bite and kill you, but you must give your kids a little space to learn on their own. Finding the proper balance is not easy.

It's a cliché, but children don't come with an instruction booklet. You, as a parent, must make your own determinations of what is right and wrong. We won't begin to tell you what you should or shouldn't do, but we will tell you what has worked for us and for our friends.

We missed a few years of camping fun from our misconception of what it would be like to camp with an infant and toddler. Regretting this loss, we hope that this book will make it possible for you to avoid the mistakes we made.

It is important to take some notes about your children's comfort, attention span, interests and objections. Check to see if your children are too warm in their sleeping bags. Perspiration and the resulting damp bag signal that you need to adjust the sleeping arrangements for your real trip. Consider unzipping the bag and using it as a comforter or as extra bedding over a cot or sleeping pad.

You may notice that your children's increased activity has them drinking or snacking more than usual. Plan for plenty of fluids and nutritious, energy foods on your actual camping trip. Much to your surprise, a typically active child may be content to sit quietly against a tree and read or observe nature. Often children are overstimulated by elements in their environment, like television, radio, video and background noise. Be alert and perceptive enough to encourage your child's pursuit of peace and quiet. Replace radios with picture-filled field guides, and substitute a personal camping journal for electronic toys when you pack for your next outing.

Chapter Three

PLANNING AND PACKING FOR THE TRIP

Once you are mentally prepared, it is time to pack up and get on the road to relaxation and adventure. Before loading your kids and dog in the back of your station wagon to head for the hills, you will need to pack the essentials for a successful trip.

This critical step can make or break your trip; don't overlook the importance of proper packing. There is more to it than just stuffing some spare clothes and extra food in a box, packing your tent and locking up the house. What you pack and how you arrange the gear will set the tone for your entire trip. Some items will need to be kept handy for on-the-road use.

NECESSARY ITEMS

Stop and think about the items you routinely use in a day. You wake up in the morning, shower, brush your teeth, go to the bathroom, possibly shave, get dressed, and eat breakfast, all in the first hour. Make a mental list of all the items used for these activities. If you plan to rough it when you go camping, you may not need all of these items, but you can bet you will need plenty of carry-along gear.

When you camp with children, you have to bring more than granola bars and sleeping bags. Keep in mind that your children may want to combine the comforts of home with instruments of exploration. They are apt to make the most popular Super Hero look lethargic. You cannot fulfill these needs with a pup tent and C-rations.

When you are creating your things-to-take list, make sure you cover all the bases. Otherwise, you may find yourself entertaining your children all day or holding their hands to get them to sleep at night. You took the first step in anticipating your children's needs with your mock camping trip. Think about the kinds of questions your children asked. What personal belongings did they want to bring to the mock camp-out?

Prized Possessions

When small hands do the packing, you never know what you may be taking to camp. You might get fifty miles down the road and find out that Fluffy the cat was smuggled aboard in a duffle bag. Many children will pack virtually the entire contents of their rooms to take with them. Some will forget to bring socks or even shoes, but will remember their stuffed bear or a box of crayons. As the parent, you must supervise, and at times intervene in, your child's packing plans. All children feel more comfortable when they bring special belongings with them on a camping trip. You should encourage this, and help them decide on one or two individual items to bring along.

Our daughter has two prized possessions, a blanket named Bubby and a favorite doll named Susan. Those two cherished friends always go camping with her. The doll stands about three feet high and Afton dresses her in hand-me-downs. When we set up camp, Afton's doll has to help. She goes with Afton to the playground, swimming, and on hikes. Susan and Bubby represent the reassurance to Afton that home is not too far away, and that the woods are not too foreign.

Afton sometimes voices her concerns through Susan or Bubby. Bubby has been afraid of the dark and Susan has heard strange noises at night. Afton will ask for a flashlight and show Bubby and Susan that there is nothing to be afraid of. In this way, she examines her own concerns and proves to herself, and her "friends," that everything is all right.

The Power of a Flashlight

The power of a flashlight can be amazing. I'm not talking about the candlepower of brightness; I'm referring to the effect it can have in calming tense children. We think all children should have their own flashlight. This one article can provide enough comfort and sense of independence to get your child through even the creepiest night.

Fisher-Price makes a great flashlight for younger children that turns itself off after about a minute. It is easy for small hands to operate, extremely rugged, and comes with white, red, and green lenses to make the darkness fun. Take your older children shopping and let them pick out their own flashlight. In this way, they will get a light that is easy for them to handle and attractive to them personally.

Creature Repellents

No camping trip would be complete without the availability of problem-solvers. Talk with your kids about the things they are apprehensive about. Heat, cold, bugs, wild animals and snakes often top the list. To appease these concerns, consider packing a battery-operated fan, hats, mittens and blankets. Bug spray, bite ointment, creature repellent, and a snakebite kit could round out your list of problem-solvers. One word of caution here: Snakebite kits can do more harm than good in untrained hands. Unless you are in an extremely remote region, you will almost always be better off to seek competent medical help than to attempt the old cut-and-suck techniques portrayed in movies and television shows.

We also bring a pump bottle of vinegar and a jar filled with beans to scare away unwanted critters. Afton shakes the jar at spooky noises and the strange smell from the vinegar deflects most small nocturnal visitors. These types of items do more to provide your children with added security in an unfamiliar place than they do to deter creature visits.

A can of air freshener is a suitable alternative to vinegar, but if you choose to use a scented spray, make sure to use it far enough away from camp not to attract animals with the aroma. The kids won't mind that the creature repellent is not close to the tent; they don't want the animals getting too close anyway.

Protection Against Ticks

Ticks are a force to be reckoned with in most states. People are quick to be on the lookout for snakes and bears, but ticks can be much more abundant and dangerous in their own way. All states, except Montana, Alaska and Hawaii, report cases of Lyme disease. This disease is serious and deserves respect and attention.

While there are antibiotics that can overcome the disease quickly with early treatment, ignored symptoms can lead to complications.

The best cure for Lyme disease is avoiding contact with the ticks that transmit the disease.

Light-colored clothing is helpful in spotting ticks before they take up residency on your skin. Strong repellents, like DEET, are effective in reducing the risk of tick bites on exposed skin, and permethrin spray applied to clothing, not skin, helps to avoid tick encounters. There is a product called Tick Release that is a poison-free, biodegradable compound meant to loosen the hold of an embedded tick. As for your pets, they can be vaccinated to reduce their risks of getting the disease.

The ticks that transmit Lyme disease can do so in the nymph stage or as an adult. In the nymph stage, these ticks are not much larger than the head of a pin, and they can be hard to detect.

By packing and wearing long pants, socks and boots, you can help protect yourself and your family from ticks. Wear shirttails and pants legs tucked in to maximize protection, and a hat gives added protection from ticks.

Clothing for Weather Variations

Consider the changes in temperatures from day to night and pack clothes that can be worn in layers. In Maine it is not uncommon for us to wear tee shirts and shorts in the afternoon and sweat suits with jackets at night. Children are particularly sensitive to changes in the temperature and may get cold faster than you do. Hats and hoods help retain body heat, and they can also offer valuable security from the sun's rays, rain, and unexpected encounters with spiderwebs and bugs.

When you are putting together your gear, include lots of extra clothes for your offspring. Rain garments are good, but somehow kids always seem to get wet, even in a poncho. It's amazing how wet they get when it hasn't even rained. Children are famous for finding streams, springs, swamps, puddles and dew. Keep this in mind, and take lots of shoes and socks. All their footwear should have textured soles, and you should include several pairs of boots.

If all of this is sounding a little obvious to you, don't skim through it or take it too lightly. We camped next to a family last spring who was only at their site overnight and had packed lightly. It snowed that night, and their children had to stay in their sleeping bags, inside the tent, because they didn't have jackets or boots to wear. Needless to say, they were not happy campers. The parents' patience was stretched to the limits, and their camping trip was cut short.

Fun Items

Next on your list of things to bring, include items to educate and entertain your family. A weekend that the weather forecaster promised to be sunny and mild can turn to raining and cold without much notice. Trust us, you do not want to be zipped into a tent or closed up in a camper with bored, anxious children who have nothing interesting to do. They will only sing campfire songs for just so long before they get ugly.

We strongly recommend puzzles, clay, beads, and other noncompetitive sources of recreation for these occasions. Cards and board games are fine when the weather is fair, but children tend to get impatient and even aggressive when Mother Nature rains on their parade. Imagine being all excited about collecting pinecones or looking for animal tracks, only to be cooped up with your entire family while puddles form outside. Look for toys or crafts your family can do together, or individually, to pass the time.

Don't Be Fooled

Don't be fooled into thinking a trailer or motorhome makes you exempt from proper planning and packing. Remember, the idea of camping as a family is not to test each member's tolerance under adverse conditions, but rather to create an environment and circumstances everyone will enjoy. The amenities of a motorhome will not exclude you from the consequences of poor packing.

We have included checklists at the end of this chapter to help you determine what to pack. These lists will limit the possibility of forgotten items. There is, however, more to packing for the trip than just gathering up what you want to take. As cars get smaller, good packing skills become more important. We are going to finish out this chapter with some tips that will enable you to pack more gear into less space.

BASIC PACKING TIPS

This section of the chapter is going to give you the basic training you need to pack your gear efficiently. As we go along, we will mention safety tips here and there, but please, always follow the manufacturer's recommendations for installations, weight limits and load placement.

Once you have completed your checklists and have all your gear stacked up next to the car, you may have trouble finding a place to put it all. We have a full-size RamCharger utility vehicle for camping trips, and we still often wish for a trailer to pull behind it. When we were camping with our travel trailer, taking along the necessities wasn't such a chore. But now that we have gone back to tent camping, the load frequently seems larger than the storage space in the vehicle.

Many people don't have full-size utility vehicles or pick-up trucks to drive off into the woods. These people are forced to ration their gear in order to get it in their cars. We had this same problem when we drove a LandCruiser and a little Jeep. Those two vehicles were fine for four-wheeling in tight spaces, but they left a lot to be desired in the cargo area.

The worst packing nightmare was going camping in the little Chevette we had many years ago. Our canoe was about twice as long as the car, and there was next to no room for anything except us on the inside.

When you are traveling with children, it always helps to keep certain items handy. Whether it is a diaper bag, a bag of potato chips or a pillow, you won't want to stop on the highway and dig through your load to get the one item you need quickly. For this reason, assemble your quick-access gear in one pile, all by itself.

Don't begin to pack anything until you have everything that needs to be packed in sight. As you develop your packing skills, you will notice that the job is much easier if you can see all the materials you have to work with before you begin.

The next step toward perfect packing requires that all items be made as controllable as possible. In some cases, this will mean having sleeping bags unrolled, so that they can be laid over a load and have the trunk lid closed on them. In other cases, it may mean packing kitchen utensils and canned food in a cardboard box for better packing procedures in the car. You will have to use some common sense as you go along.

Once you get used to packing, the process will go quickly and easily. The first few times, however, will not progress so rapidly. You will undoubtedly have to pull things out and repack them a time or two to get the job done right. Don't despair, it will get easier each time you do it.

When you have all your stuff stacked near your vehicle, take a good look at it. Think of your cargo area as the outline of a puzzle and the gear as pieces of that puzzle. Look for boxes with shapes that will naturally go together. Avoid packing items without boxes whenever possible. For example, if you will be taking a lantern, pack it in the box you bought it in. The box will allow you to work with flat, solid surfaces, and this is much easier than dealing with round, slippery finishes.

For obvious reasons, pack heavy gear on the bottom and lighter goods on top. Use plastic cups rather than glasses for drinking. Not only is the plastic safer in the campsite, it will not break on the trip. If you have a lot of small, loose items to deal with, pack them in a cardboard box. The type of boxes used to store file folders work great, and they only cost about a dollar apiece.

If you will be loading the back of a station wagon or utility vehicle, be careful how high you pack your load. Not only will tall loads block your visibility in the rear window, the load could be thrown forward if you have to hit the brakes quickly. This can result in some serious injuries. It is possible to install wire fencing and other types of barriers between the load and passengers if you need that extra height to make the load fit. Be sure, however, that your safety barrier is secure and will stand up to an auto accident.

If your children are small, you can use the floor space in the back seat to carry extra gear. This is a great place to pack your quick-access needs, and the floor provides ample width to accommodate your tent. You can even unroll your sleeping bags and foam pads and lay them over the load on the floor. Your children can use the soft foam or sleeping bags as a footrest.

If you will be packing fuel for a cooking stove or lantern, make sure the container is capped tightly and packed securely. It is best to pack such flammable or potentially explosive items as far away from the passengers as possible, and it doesn't hurt to surround them with blankets or similar padding to reduce the risk of punctures.

When you are taking a cooler on the trip, but don't plan to ice it down until you get to camp, you can pack gear inside the cooler. If you will be camping near a grocery store, you may want to buy your food there, rather than packing it for the long haul. It may cost a little more, but it will conserve space when you don't have to carry it along with all the rest of your camping equipment.

We have found that duffle bags offer more packing flexibility with clothes than suitcases do. Since clothes are soft, they can often be squeezed in around other parts of your load. This not only maximizes the utilization of available space, the clothes firm up the load and keep it from shifting.

If you decide to take a playpen or fold-down crib, you might do well to attach it to a roof rack. A trunk rack or even a bicycle carrier can also be used to haul such bulky items. If you elect to cover an outside load with a tarp, be advised, tarps are often loosened by the wind they encounter on the road. Tie the tarp securely and check it periodically. You wouldn't want it to fly off and cover some other motorist's windshield.

Stuffed animals and similar soft toys can be stuck in between the load, like clothes, to maximize the use of your space and to stabilize your load.

Overlooked Storage Areas
There are many overlooked storage areas in most vehicles. We've already told you how to make use of floor space when your children don't have long legs, and now we're going to give you some other ideas.

- Board games and other relatively flat objects can be placed under the seats. In doing this, make sure the items will not slide forward and interfere with your use of the brake pedal, gas pedal, or clutch pedal.

- If your vehicle has a console compartment or a glove compartment, don't overlook their capacity. These areas are great for small, quick-access items.

• There should be adequate space between the outside edges of the rear seat and the car's outside shell to slide books, games, maps, collapsible water jugs and similar items.

• If your spare tire has a cover over it, remove the cover and investigate the space possibilities. You are likely to find a hollow in the tire that can hold a small backpack of goodies.

• Seats that have pockets on the back of them offer a good place for packing quick-access needs. Unless you have a full load of children, a portion of the seat they are riding on can be used for transporting soft items. This is a great place for those stuffed animals and pillows.

• If you are really starved for space, you can buy a net that looks something like a hammock to attach to the inside wall of your vehicle. These cargo nets can carry a lot of lightweight stuff, and they don't cost much.

• If you are packing a trailer, whether it is a utility trailer, travel trailer or pop-up trailer, pack your load evenly and don't exceed the trailer's gross-weight rating. If the weight of the load is not distributed evenly, the trailer will not tow properly, and safety risks can result.

• Cartop carriers are great for extending your cargo space, but it's awfully embarrassing and dangerous to have one fly off the roof of your car when going down the road. If you intend to use a cartop carrier, roof rack, or wheel-less trailer, make sure the unit is securely and properly attached to your vehicle. You should also cover the load with a cargo net, or some type of cover, to assure that the load will not blow out of the carrier. As an added safety precaution when using a hardtop carrier, it is a good idea to tie a rope around the carrier to keep the lid closed in case the latch fails.

Look over the checklists to familiarize yourself with items you may wish to include on your next camping trip, and then turn to chapter five to find out how getting there can be half the fun.

QUICK-ACCESS CHECKLIST

ITEM	HAVE	NEED	PACKED
Changing bag (baby)			
Snacks			
Sticker books			
Writing paper			
Pens/pencils/crayons/markers			
Storybooks			
Travel bingo cards			
Work/activity/coloring books			
Laptop travel desk			
Travel map			
Pillow			
Auto sunshade for window			
Cool drinks			
Pacifier			
Rattles/baby toys			
Stuffed animals			
Paper towels			
Towelettes			

GENERAL CAMPING GEAR CHECKLIST

ITEM	HAVE	NEED	PACKED
Backpacks			
Fire-starting tinder			
Child carrier			
Day pack			
Tent, poles, stakes			
Tarp for under tent floor			
Sleeping bags			
Extra blankets			
Air mattresses/foam pads			
Pillows			
Heavy work gloves			
Lantern & spare mantles			
Camp stove			
Lantern & stove fuel			
Flashlights			
Batteries/bulbs			
Folding chairs			
Folding table			
Portable toilet			
Camp saw			
Ax			
Fire extinguisher			
Water purifier			
Collapsible water jugs			
Rope and twine			
Compass			
Topographical maps			
Whistles			
Knives—pocket/sheath			

PERSONAL ITEMS CHECKLIST

ITEMS TO KEEP IN CAMP BAG	HAVE	NEED	PACKED
Sunglasses			
Shampoo			
Comb/hairbrush			
Toothbrushes & paste			
Dental floss			
Deodorant			
Shaving kit			
Towels			
Soap			
Towelettes			
Lip balm			
Hair bands/ribbons			
Sanitary napkins/tampons			
Toilet paper			
Nail clippers			
ITEMS TO PACK EACH TRIP			
Daily medications			
Eyeglasses & case			
Contact lens kit			
Birth control devices			

INDIVIDUAL CHILD'S CHECKLIST

ITEMS KIDS CAN PACK	HAVE	NEED	PACKED
Stuffed animals			
Magnifying glass			
Playing cards			
Plaster for casting tracks			
Work/activity/coloring books			
Collection containers			
Toy figures			
Writing paper			
Pens/pencils/crayons/markers			
Travel and board games			
Water gun			
Ball			
Harmonica/kazoo			
Frisbee			
Books (stories/novels)			
Safety scissors			
Glue/glue sticks			
Log books/diaries			
Pogo stick			
Clay/dough			
Beads and string			
Tape			
Construction paper			
Butterfly net			
THINGS FOR PARENTS TO PACK			
Camera gear			
Field guidebooks			
Binoculars			
Fishing gear			

The Parent's Guide to Camping With Children

CHILD'S CLOTHING CHECKLIST

ITEM	HAVE	NEED	PACKED
Hats/caps			
Earmuffs			
Gloves/mittens			
Raincoats/ponchos			
Boots (wet weather)			
Boots (hiking)			
Socks			
Long pants			
Shorts			
Underwear			
Insulated underwear			
Shirts			
Sweatshirts			
Hooded sweatshirts			
Sleepwear			
Jackets			
Coats			
Shoes			

INFANT/TODDLER CHECKLIST

ITEM	HAVE	NEED	PACKED
Diapers			
Baby powder			
Baby oil			
Rubber pants			
Baby bottles/liners			
Bottle nipples			
Towelettes			
Changing cloth			
Mosquito netting			
Pacifier			
Playpen/portable crib			
Music box			
Assorted toys			
Diaper rash lotion			
Soft books & toys			
Hats/bonnets			
Sleeper suits			
Bibs			
Assorted clothes			
Shoes			
Socks			
Cold-weather suits			
Petroleum jelly			
Training pants			
Formula			
Diaper pail			
Teething ring			
Blanket & pillow			

KITCHEN ITEMS CHECKLIST

ITEM	HAVE	NEED	PACKED
Lighter/waterproof matches			
Windscreen for stove			
Sharp knife			
Eating utensils			
Cooking utensils			
Pots & pans			
Bowls			
Can openers			
Cutting board			
Ice chest			
Aluminum foil			
Reclosable plastic bags			
Paper towels			
Scrub pads			
Dishpan			
Dish detergent			
Food containers			
Pot holders			
Sponge			
Fire grill			
Coffeepot			
Cups & plastic tumblers			
Plastic jars with lids			
Strainer			
Trash bags & ties			
Potato masher			
Skillet/frying pan			

FIRST-AID AND EMERGENCY CHECKLIST

ITEM	HAVE	NEED	PACKED
Headache/pain tablets			
Insect-bite medicine			
Rash/irritation lotion			
Bandages			
Gauze rolls			
Gauze pads			
Ace bandage			
Butterfly bandages			
Hydrogen peroxide			
Instant cold pack			
Tweezers			
Mirror			
Sterile wipes			
Antacid tablets			
Motion-sickness tablets			
Diarrhea medicine			
Laxative			
Foot powder			
Baby powder			
Adhesive tape			
Blister pads			
Dental topical painkiller			
Topical painkiller for skin			
Deep-heating rub			
Alcohol			
Salt tablets			
Scissors			
Antiseptic			
Cough medicine			

FIRST-AID AND EMERGENCY CHECKLIST (continued)

ITEM	HAVE	NEED	PACKED
Eye drops			
Decongestant			
Needles			
Thread			
Single-edge razor blades			
Thermometer (not glass)			
Snakebite kit			
Cold tablets			
Tourniquet			
Baking soda			
Water-purification tablets			
Space blanket			
Flashlight			
Safety pins			
Cotton balls			
Cotton swabs			
Ipecac syrup			
Throat lozenges			
Lighter/waterproof matches			
Twine			
Sunscreen			
Insect repellent			
First-aid instruction book			

PET CHECKLIST

ITEM	HAVE	NEED	PACKED
Carrier			
Leash			
Food bowl			
Water bowl			
Food			
Fresh flea collar			
Tick repellent			
Tie-out rope			
Vaccination information			
Tags and collar			
Halter			

BEFORE YOU LEAVE CHECKLIST

ITEM	NEED TO DO	DONE
Check oil in vehicle		
Check washer fluid in vehicle		
Check fuel in vehicle		
Check tire pressure for vehicle		
Check thermostat in house		
Make sure stove and oven are off		
Make sure all pets are secure		
Put map and directions in car		
Check cash and credit cards		
Pack all permits (fishing/fire/etc.)		
Leave word with relatives on trip plan		
Check spare tire in vehicle		
Check to be sure load is secure		
Close windows in house		
Lock windows and doors		
Unplug the toaster		
Turn off the coffeepot		
Unplug the curling iron		
Set automatic light timers		
Make arrangements to hold mail delivery		
Make arrangements to hold paper delivery		
Check all other checklists		

Chapter Four

PETS, STUFFED ANIMALS, BIKES AND OTHER SPECIAL CONSIDERATIONS

Pets, stuffed animals, bikes and other special considerations all come into play when you start camping with kids. You have probably been very surprised at the types of items kids feel are necessities for a camping trip.

Pets are another issue all unto their own. Whether you leave them at home, place them at a kennel, or take them with you, special arrangements will certainly be needed. Advance planning will usually resolve the potential problems caused by pets when it comes to a family camping trip.

As a loving parent, you want your children to be happy. The problem comes in finding ways to tell your kids that they can't take this or that on the trip. What started out to be a great family getaway can turn nasty when a child is denied the chance to bring Leo, the giant stuffed lion, along. You know Leo is too big to pack in the car with all the necessary camping gear, but how do you explain that to little Tyler?

Saying no to children is seldom easy for parents, but there are times when it is necessary not to give in. Children tend to view camping trips a little differently than adults do. To kids, the trip is a gala event and they feel that all the favorite toys and pets should be taken along for the good time. There are ways, however, to convince children not to take certain toys and animals on the camping trip without breaking their hearts.

DECIDING WHAT TO TAKE

Deciding what to take on a camping trip is not an easy assignment for young children. If you simply ask your children to pick out what they want to take on the trip and stack it in the living room, there is a good chance the room will fill up before you put any regular camping gear in the pile. For this reason, you have to help your children separate their needs from their desires.

Needs

There are certain items that most children will place under the category of needs: a favorite book, a snuggly blanket, a worn-out stuffed animal, or any number of other things. Since you will be taking care of the essential needs for the camping trip, your children's lists should be short. It is, however, important that you allow them to take a few items that they feel are mandatory cargo.

Desires

If you are making a list of needs and desires with your children, most items will fall into the desires category. Bicycles, remote-control cars and boats, dolls, action figures, and anything else they might own are likely to be listed as desires. To preserve room in the family vehicle, you must work with the children to make both lists as reasonable as possible.

Limit the List

One way to handle the problem of taking too much stuff is to put a limit on the list of items selected for the trip. In other words, you might tell the children that each one of them is allowed to take up to six personal items. These would include items from both the needs and the desires list. This approach works to some extent, though you might also have to put size limitations on the items.

Our daughter has a dollhouse that is so big she can crawl into it. The house has two stories and would not fit in the trunk of a compact car. Obviously, something of this magnitude is not a good choice for taking on a camping trip. Her dolls, however, are small, easy to pack, and don't take up much room. Based on just these two items, we would be much better off to let Afton bring ten dolls rather than one dollhouse. This is just one example, but it demonstrates the problems of limiting the number of items a child can take.

Talk It Out

If you talk it out with your children, there are many ways to explain why certain items, like huge dollhouses, cannot go along on the camping excursion. Children who are too young to understand are also too young to be demanding that a truckload of toys go on the trip, so for this group of kids you will not be faced with the same problems parents with older children might have.

One of the best approaches to the problem of taking too much stuff is to prioritize the items. When you ask your children to select the items to be taken on the trip, ask them to rank the things on a scale of one to ten in terms of importance. Explain that once the car is loaded with all the necessary gear, you will allow as many toys to be taken as there is room. Start loading the car with the most important items. When the car fills up, your children will understand that there is no more room but that their most important possessions are already loaded. The remainder of the items on the desires list can be left at home with a clear conscience. This approach has always worked well for us.

INVOLVE YOUR CHILDREN

Involve your children in the decision-making process of what to take and what to leave behind. You've already seen a few examples of how you can get the kids involved, but let's look at some other ways that will work.

Older Children

Older children are usually the easiest to get involved in the decision-making process. It is not too difficult for a teenager to understand that a mountain bike, a guitar, a boom box, and a private tent may be a little much to expect to take on a weekend trip. While teens are able to understand the limitations of space, they may not accept any better than a six-year-old the fact that certain things can't go. Don't overlook this possibility when working through a packing ordeal with a teenager.

A little game-playing of your own can work with older kids. While we don't have older children, we both have been very active with teenage brothers, sisters and cousins. During these times, we have learned a bit about dealing with the older group. It also helps to remember how you thought as a teenager.

Suppose you had a teenage son who wanted to bring an all-terrain vehicle (ATV), a canoe, and a mountain bike with him on a weekend outing. The canoe can be tied on top of the vehicle, the bike can be mounted on a bike rack, but the ATV requires pulling a trailer that you don't want to be bothered with. How would you eliminate the ATV from the picture?

One way might be to explain that you are not sure if the area you will be camping in will allow the use of an ATV. Explain how that by trailering the ATV behind the car, you might be prevented from entering the wilderness area or the park. This one approach is probably all that would be needed.

If the boy still insists on taking the ATV, you might be able to discourage him by discussing the dry weather you've been having and the potential fire risk of taking the ATV off road.

Since you will only be camping for a short time, you could play your cards on that bet, and point out how there will not be adequate time to use a canoe, a bike and an ATV on this trip.

A more straightforward approach would be to level with your son. Tell him that you don't want to be slowed down by the trailer and that you are going into unfamiliar surroundings where you feel uncomfortable towing the ATV. Honesty often works very well.

If worse comes to worse, you will have to invoke your parental power and make a flat denial of the request. This won't gain you any popularity, but if you have taken the time to explain your concerns, the child should understand and accept your decision.

Younger Children

Younger children typically are more interested in taking a large volume of toys, stuffed animals and other possessions than older children are. They are also sometimes easier to deal with in the denial stage. Little kids seem to accept their parent's wishes better than teenagers.

If you don't want to be the bad guy, you must find a way to let your children decide for themselves what to take and what to leave at home. This is not as hard as you might think.

The key to a happy child is involvement in the problem-solving stage. We have had occasions when it was obvious that some of what Afton wanted to take on a trip was not feasible. Our solution to the problem has been to ask for her help. We explain what the problem is and ask Afton how she would solve it. Her answers, with only a few exceptions, have always been good enough to make the trip work out. Typically, Afton will look over the pile of gear to be packed and make recommendations on what should be left behind. Since she is making the decision herself, she doesn't become angry with either one of us.

PETS

Pets can be a serious concern for people leaving home to go camping. Who will feed the animals you leave behind? Will you have to pay to board the animals in a kennel? Should you take your pets with you on the camping trip? If you decide to take the animals with you, what special arrangements will have to made? Let's examine your options.

Leaving the Animals at Home

Leaving the animals at home is easier for some people than it is for others. Asking a parakeet to take care of itself for a long weekend is not a big deal, but asking a dog to do the same thing is more complicated. Cats can be left for several days without problems, but what about the pet pig? There is no question, some animals are easier to leave at home, unattended, than others are.

If you happen to have friends or relatives close by to care for the animals while you are away, leaving them at home is not such a problem. But what if there isn't anyone available to feed and water the dog? Unlike cats, dogs tend to eat all of the food they are given at one time. This makes it very difficult indeed to leave the pooch unattended for several days at a time.

Many cities have companies that will take care of pets for a price. If you need someone to feed and water your animals, check the local phone directory to see if such services are available in your area. Your babysitter is another possible option. He or she may be willing to look after the pets.

Boarding the Animals

Boarding the animals is a good way to get around the pet problem, but it can get expensive. If you can't arrange to have someone you trust stop in to feed and water your pet, a kennel is probably your best bet.

Dealing With Your Child's Concern

Dealing with your child's concern for the family pet while you are gone may be your biggest hurdle to clear in the animal dilemma. Kids often worry about their pets in the same ways that parents feel concern for their children. If your child is worried about a pet, don't take the issue too lightly.

When we have gone on long trips, Afton has frequently showed concern for her pets. It has usually been a combination of not wanting to be away from the animals and being afraid something bad would happen to them. We have gotten around the fear factor by making sure Afton is comfortable with the person selected to care for the pets.

Take the time to talk to your children about how the pets will be taken care of, where they will be, and how they will be better off staying behind. Even a young child will understand most, if not all, of what you are saying. Once you are on your way to camp, the animals are not likely to become a topic of conversation until bedtime or until the child becomes bored. Expect a little crying during these times, and be prepared to talk your child through the first few separations from the pets.

Taking the Pets With You

Taking the pets with you can produce mixed results. There will be the joy and happiness of having your pet with you, but there will also be the inconvenience of having to deal with the pet under unusual circumstances. For example, you may want to go to a beach where dogs are not allowed; what will you do with the pup then? If you decide to go into town for dinner, what will you do with the pet? These types of problems arise frequently when camping with pets.

Not all campgrounds allow pets; this is something you should be sure to check on before taking the family pet along. If you take a cat or dog into strange surroundings, there is always a possibility that the pet will run off and get lost. Depending upon where you will be camping, there may be animals or birds of prey that could put your pet at risk. Also, a playful puppy can do a lot of damage to a nylon tent. There are many good reasons for leaving pets at home.

Should the Family Pet Go Along for the Ride?

Should the family pet go along for the ride? The answer to this question is a personal one. When we are tent camping, we never take the pets. On the occasions when we camp in a cabin, Afton's dog generally goes along with us. The cats always stay at home, since they are able to take care of themselves. Our rule is that Trinket, the puppy, can come camping with us if we are staying in a cabin or the travel trailer, but not if we are tenting.

Before you decide to take your pet, consider all the complications and potential problems associated with doing so. In many cases, the trip will be more enjoyable without the responsibility of a pet. However, some pets are better than others about traveling and behaving themselves. Clearly, the correct answer to the question lies with you, your child, and your pet.

Chapter Five

GETTING THERE CAN BE HALF THE FUN

Is it true that getting there can be half the fun of camping? Many parents would take a strong stand in opposition to the suggestion that traveling for an extended time with children is fun. While you may never consider the trek to camp in a car fun, there are ways to make life easier for yourself.

A lot of people find driving, with or without kids in the car, to be somewhat less than desirable. Spending several hours on the road to get to your favorite camping spot may be worth the effort, but it rarely seems to be an enjoyable part of the camping experience. Factor in a crying baby or a loud child, and you have all the makings for a major headache.

Asking an excited child to sit quietly for a two-hour ride is not only ineffective, it is not a reasonable request. To make the ride more enjoyable for yourself and your child, you will have to put forth a little effort. It helps to have your spouse along for the ride, but there is much you can do, even when you're the only adult in the car, to take the edge off the traveling.

We have developed numerous ways to keep Afton entertained on long drives. Feel free to use our suggestions or to modify them to suit your personal needs.

SONGS

My family loved to sing on road trips. We had some old favorites like "Whoops, There Goes Another Rubber Tree Plant." Songs you could sing in rounds were always fun. Each of us would cover our ears so we wouldn't start singing someone else's part. There is great fun in making up lines to old songs, or singing songs like "Old MacDonald" where everyone takes a turn adding a line to the song. Rhyming songs are enjoyable for people of all ages. We used to sing, "The Ants Go Marching One By One," and each person would try to come up with something silly for the littlest ant to stop for.

If you don't know the song, it essentially goes, "The ants go marching one by one, hurrah, hurrah. The ants go marching one by one, hurrah, hurrah. The ants go marching one by one; the little one . . ." and then we would make up what he did such as ". . . the little one stopped to chew some gum, and they all go marching down into the ground, to get out of the rain." Then the ants go marching two by two and so on. There are plenty of rhyming songs like "This Old Man" and "Michael Finnegan." Action songs are also good for long rides. Smaller children enjoy "Where Is Thumbkin" and "Head, Shoulders, Knees, And Toes." When the singing ends, you can also play games like "Simon Says." Mothers love to use the ploy, "Simon says be very quiet!"

THE REST OF THE STORY

Along the same line as singing rounds and adding verses to songs, is the idea of making up stories. Get everyone involved by asking each person to add to the story as it develops. For example, the first person starts off with "Once there was a big dragon," the next person continues with "who lived on the top of a tall mountain," the next person adds "and he loved to eat pepperoni pizzas." Young and old can join in the fun. Don't be surprised if your family is in hysterics by the time the dragon is done battling Captain Pizza and flies home with fair Maiden Mozzarella to live happily ever after.

THE COLOR GAME

The color game is effective for children of almost any age. In this game, the judge (usually a parent) stipulates a color to look for. Children keep their eyes peeled for something of the proper color. For example, if the color was red, a stop sign would be a suitable target. If the color was yellow, a yield sign would do. When the color is brown, a cow or a car might fit the bill.

Score can be kept as the selected colors are changed. The first person to get ten correct colors might win a prize. The prize could be a piece of candy, a sticker-type award, or any number of other rewards.

As a variation of the color game, the game can be played based on letters. For example, the judge could tell contestants to look for an object where the first letter in its name is a "B." A bus would be one possible winner in this game.

BINGO
Commercial bingo cards are available for kids on the go. These cards are marked with traffic signs, types of vehicles, and other objects likely to be seen on the road. As a child spots an appropriate item, the square on the card is covered. The first player to complete a bingo wins. If you want to prolong the game, you can play blackout bingo. This is where all the squares on the board must be covered to produce a winner.

THE GUESSING GAME
The guessing game is easy to play on the road. There are many possible variations of this game. Afton's favorite version is where one person makes a sound and the other person tries to guess what kind of animal makes the same sound. You might create a game where each occupant of the vehicle would guess what color the next car to approach will be or what color the next house you pass will be. Score can be kept for correct answers and rewards can be given to the winner.

What Am I?
This variation of the guessing game involves picking an animal or thing which a player describes in stages. For example, begin by saying "I am brown, what am I?" Each person then takes a turn looking for clues, asking if the thing is alive, is it an animal, is it big, and so on. Teenagers will come up with some incredible things to be. In this game, kids have been the planet Mars, a dinosaur fossil and a duck-billed platypus. This game is fun for all ages. Our five-year-old kept us guessing for twenty minutes before we figured out she was a car seat.

BARNEY THE MOSQUITO
One of Afton's all-time favorite games to play has been Barney the Mosquito. Barney is a finger-play game which simply uses the index finger of one of our hands. Barney is a friendly mosquito who doesn't bite, and he likes Afton. Barney has a buddy named Friend

Bird. Friend Bird is one of our hands. Friend Bird never eats Barney, but he does enjoy eating the bad, biting mosquitos. When Afton hears a humming sound and sees just an index finger moving in on her, she knows it is Barney. If she sees a flapping hand coming toward her, she knows it's Friend Bird. Should she hear a humming sound and see a thumb and index finger moving to make a pinching motion, it is a sure sign that a bad mosquito is coming in. Barney fights the bad mosquitos and Friend Bird eats them to protect Afton. This may sound like a silly game, but we have been playing it off and on for a couple of years, and Afton still loves it.

PORTABLE DESKS

Portable desks, the type with sandbags that sit in your lap, or even breakfast trays, provide a stable surface for children to work on. The work can be drawing, coloring or whatever. Clipboards also work well. Provide your children with ample resources such as markers, crayons, stickers and colored pencils, and they will keep themselves busy for quite a while.

Tape and Glue

You might be amazed at how entertaining a roll of tape is to a child. Some tape and some paper may be all you need to keep your child happy on the trip. Afton once spent over an hour covering the top of her plastic travel desk with tape. She meticulously concealed every inch of the surface. When she was done, she spent another fifteen minutes carefully lifting the tape off in one large sheet.

Many parents are hesitant to bring glue in the car because it is so hard to control. There are two kinds of manageable glue that we pack on every trip. The first is a wet glue stick with a spongy applicator tip. Gentle pressure on the paper's surface brings just the right amount of glue out and avoids dripping. The other glue looks very much like lip balm. You twist the bottom to raise the thick, tacky glue. There is even a purple glue stick that goes on the paper purple, but dries clear. Small children enjoy this product's disappearing act.

CAMPING JOURNAL

One of the best things you can do for your children is to provide them with the materials to construct their own camping journal.

You will need a spiral or loose-leaf notebook, reference materials, old magazines, scissors, tape, glue sticks, markers and crayons.

The purpose of the journal is twofold. Initially, it will give your kids an interesting project to work on in the car. Finally, it will become the means for your child to record and keep camping experiences. As you travel, talk with your family about the kinds of things they can expect to encounter while camping. Ask the kids what they think they will find in the forest or at the beach. Listen carefully as they describe trees, animals, water and other elements. You can begin to get an idea of what is most intriguing to them, and also what they may be feeling apprehensive about.

Next, have them look through the magazines and cut out pictures of things they want to look for and learn more about while they are camping. When the cutting and pasting is done, see what they have in the journal. One popular item is trees, possibly because there are so many in outdoor magazines. You can increase your family's curiosity by talking about some of the interesting qualities of trees.

Prepare your children to collect various leaves and match them to pictures in field guides. They also will be able to do rubbings to record different tree bark textures. As you discuss the possibilities, your children can make additional drawings or notations in their journals of experiments to try or clues to look for in the field.

The journal is an invaluable part of a camping trip. It will spark your children's imagination and curiosity. They will take a hard look at the world around them, and ask to learn about their surroundings. Keeping a journal gives your children an appreciation of nature and they are less likely to carelessly destroy their environment while camping.

If you have a rainy day during your trip, your family can go over the information in their journals and exchange ideas and fun facts. What starts off as a way to keep your kids occupied in the car will become an enduring album of memories and knowledge which your children will treasure. They can make a new journal each time they travel and start their own reference library.

FREQUENT STOPS

No matter how entertaining you make the trip, your family will need to stop and take some breaks to stretch their legs. Toddlers particularly need frequent stops to get out and move around. Most infant car seats are not very comfortable after a couple of hours. Try to schedule periodic stops which include exercise, trips to the bathroom, and refreshments. I know how imposing this can be if you have a large family—by the time you get everyone's shoes on, and herd them in and out of the bathroom, you may feel as though you lost an hour of travel time. However, you will make your life easier if everyone knows when they will have a chance to get drinks, run or walk around a bit, and go to the bathroom. Be prepared for the possibility of car sickness as well. My parents always gave me medicine before a long trip, or they knew we would be making unexpected stops along the way!

You will eliminate a great deal of badgering from your children and the number of "When will we be there?" and "Are we there yet?" questions will decrease when you schedule rest stops. Most of the time these questions are really statements of boredom or discomfort. A few breaths of fresh air will benefit everyone.

Your children can also take the opportunity at information booths to gather pamphlets about the areas you are traveling through or to. Save these brochures to help identify points of interest to include in your next trip.

You might also consider starting the first leg of a long trip early in the morning. This works well if you have toddlers who barely wake up when you carry them from the house to the car, and will then sleep for the first several hours of the trip. The downside to this approach with older children is that waking up in the car interferes with their morning rituals which usually include brushing teeth and hair, breakfast, and going to the bathroom.

Traveling late into the night causes the same dilemmas. Some older children will be so excited about the trip that they cannot fall asleep in the car and will be bored and cranky with nothing to do during the twilight hours. Use your judgment when choosing to travel early or drive late into the night.

Well, there you have it. You are now privy to our traveling secrets. Now, let's move on to the next chapter, and see about making camp.

Chapter Six

MAKING CAMP

Making camp can be a very enjoyable part of camping. It can also be a most miserable time. What makes the difference? Part of the equation is having the right tools and equipment. The other part is having cooperative kids. If your children are pulling at you, whining, or running wild about the woods, making camp can become a nightmare.

When you first arrive at your campsite, the kids are going to be excited and full of stored-up energy. This combination can make for some tedious times when making camp. How do you tell a twelve-year-old boy he can't wet a line in the lake until camp is made? Can you really expect a five-year-old girl to put aside her fascination with the dozen cute, cuddly, pet bunnies that inhabit the campground long enough for you to erect a tent and stock it with camping supplies? It is hard enough for adults to throttle their excitement with a new place long enough to make camp; for children, it's even harder.

As a parent, you should want your children to be excited about the campsite you have selected. If they are not bouncing with energy and anticipation, you've probably failed at finding a great spot. On the other hand, you need the children to cooperate with you in setting up your camp. How will you manage to accomplish both goals? You will do so by following the advice we are about to give you.

ALL CAMPERS MUST ORGANIZE

All campers have a certain amount of work that must be done before their camp is established. Cabin campers don't have as much to do as tenters, but the car still has to be unloaded, and items have to be stored in the cabin.

Campers with motorhomes have the least responsibility for establishing their camp. They park the land yacht, level it up, and off they go.

Travel trailers are similar to motorhomes in their convenience. The trailer is parked and leveled, and then it is time to play.

Pop-up campers have to park their trailer, level it, and unfold it. Then there is the transfer of gear from the car to the trailer and the stowing of goods that were transported in the floor of the trailer. This is certainly more work than is required with the other types of camping we have just talked about, but nothing to compare with what tent campers have to contend with.

Tent campers have their work cut out for them. They must unload the car, find a suitable spot for their tent, erect the tent (which isn't always easy), load the tent with their stuff, make cooking facilities, and so on. Tenters will benefit most from this chapter, but every camper will save precious time in establishing camp by using the following tips.

ARRIVING EARLY

Arriving early in the day is one of the best ways to take the edge off of setting up camp. If you get to your campsite early, you can let the kids explore the area for awhile before making camp. This gives you a chance to stretch out muscles that may be sore from driving, while your children burn off their pent-up energy.

After the kids have had an hour or so to roam around, you can call in the troops to begin making camp. This short recess between traveling and setting up camp can make all the difference in the world.

As a word of caution, don't put off making camp for too long. Procrastination can lead to a dampening experience if the weather changes quickly. Also, if you allow the break between driving and making camp to run on too long, neither you nor the kids may be in the mood for getting to the work at hand. If the fun lasts for more than an hour or so, it can be difficult to get it stopped long enough to make camp during daylight hours. And, if you think setting up a camp is no fun under normal conditions, you certainly won't want to tackle the chore after dark.

ASSIGNING DUTIES

Assigning duties to your children is one way to get them involved in the set-up aspect of camping. Some children will not want to take an active part in the set-up phase, but many will relish the opportunity to help Mom and Dad make camp. There are times, however, when the help from a child makes the job much longer, so allow for this delay when you are planning the amount of time needed to get situated.

Most children will be glad to help in setting up their camp. They will derive pleasure and pride from the job. Whether it is driving tent stakes in the ground, collecting firewood, or rolling out the awning on the RV, kids love to accomplish goals that they feel proud of. It is up to you to make the duty both a desirable deed and an activity that the child will be praised for and proud of. How will you accomplish this? Well, let us show you.

ESTABLISHING CAMP

Establishing camp with the help of your children can be a lot of fun. If you make something of a game out of the chore, kids will love making camp.

Setting Up a Tent

Setting up a tent is probably the most difficult thing you have to do when making camp with children. Tents can be complicated to erect, and the help of too many small hands can make the job turn from bad to worse. The first step toward avoiding this problem is the purchase of an easy-to-set-up tent, like an umbrella tent.

If you have a tent that is equipped with built-in tent poles that are shock-corded together, the whole tent can be popped open in less than five minutes, and it can be done by just one adult. This leaves your spouse free to occupy the children while you open up the tent.

If you have a quick-fix tent, you may still be faced with a youngster who wants to help. One solution to keeping the child happy and at the same time out of your way is to allow the child to install the ground cover while you are opening the tent. If the child is large enough to walk, he or she can spread out the ground cover.

When you need more time to get the tent open than will be allowed by the child simply spreading out a tarp, there is plan B. Explain to your child how important it is to remove all rocks and sticks from the tent site. Surely, by the time he or she can pick up all the rocks, sticks, acorns, and other hard objects, you can have the tent opened and ready to put into place. This tactic works even for a single parent, since it keeps the child close at hand and under direct supervision, without being in the way.

Once the ground has been cleared and the ground cover is in place, your child can help you put the tent into place. Next, if the child is old enough, let the youngster drive in the tent stakes. Once the stakes are in place, you can secure the hold-down strings and the fly.

Unloading the Car

Unloading the car and loading the tent or stocking the cabin is another activity you can involve the children in. There should be plenty of items that are light enough for small children to handle. In fact, you can make sure of this when you pack your gear. Remember to keep some of the boxes, bags and other containers kid-sized.

You can either have the child stack all of the items in a common place for you to sort through later, or you can direct the young camper to specific places for the various items. This not only keeps the kids under your watchful eye during a necessary part of making camp, it saves you trips to and from the car.

Give Blanky the Tour

Once you have all your gear in the tent or cabin, you can buy yourself some more time by having children give blanky or teddy the tour. In the case of cabin camping, there will be plenty of interior adventures for your children and their favorite stuffed animals or blankets to explore. When tent camping, you can let the children explore within the established camp boundaries while you make provisions for cooking, setting up tables, or whatever other outside set-ups are needed.

A Camera

A camera can go a long way in keeping most kids occupied while you tend to necessary set-up chores. Make it a regular routine for your child to take photos of every new campsite you visit. An inexpensive camera and a roll of film is a small price to pay for the peace it allows you during the set-up stage of camping.

Take Turns

Take turns with your spouse in setting up your camp. One of you can be responsible for unloading the car and the other for putting the gear away. This will divide the child-watching duty and the set-up work evenly.

Pack Toys Last

If you pack toys last, they will be the first items to be unloaded. Get the toys out of the car first, and you have something for your children to play with while you finish getting the camping gear out.

A Visit to the Community Room

If you are camping in a commercial campground, a visit to the community room can keep your children occupied for awhile. There are usually games for the kids to play and lots of items to be examined in campground community rooms.

Mock Television Shows

If your child is old enough to have a few favorite television shows, you may be able to make a game of mocking them with the set-up chores. For example, our daughter went through a phase where her favorite show was about a family that was forced to live in wilderness conditions with limited supplies. We exploited this fascination with the show whenever it was time to set up camp.

When we went tent camping, we would pretend we were the family from the television show. Setting up the tent was the equivalent of the television characters building their tree house. Unloading the truck was similar to the television family bringing provisions in from the woods. When playing this type of game with Afton, she rarely wanted to stop setting up camp.

Role-playing can work for kids of all ages that have an interest in the outdoors. I still envision myself as a mountain man right out of the movies from time to time, and I believe everyone, regardless of age, has some image that they enjoy dreaming about.

If you take the time to play along with the fantasies that your children have about the outdoors, you can turn their fantasies into your good fortune when it comes to setting up camp.

Merit Badges

If you were ever into scouting activities, you must remember merit badges. These were symbols of achievement that children wore to show their peers how accomplished they were at various tasks. Both of us were involved with scouting, and we both remember the pride we had in sporting our colorful patches and badges. This memory has led us to another victory in the battle of setting up camp with kids.

Instead of a typical reward system where a child gets a candy bar for doing something, we use a merit badge system. Afton collects badges, stickers and patches for her accomplishments. This is better for her teeth than candy, and they are lasting rewards that instill pride in her.

You can either create or buy your merit badges and award them for various accomplishments that your children make. For example, one of the badges could be for driving in all the tent stakes without help from a parent. Another badge might indicate the child's prowess at cooking supper or building the campfire. Your imagination is the only limit to what the merit badge system can be used for.

If you make a game out of making camp, your children will not only participate in a helpful way, they will enjoy it. With such a system, both you and your children will be more refreshed, relaxed and satisfied with the task of making camp.

Chapter Seven

CAMPSITE ACTIVITIES KIDS ENJOY

This chapter is going to give you some fun ideas that go well with camping. Camping is great fun all by itself, but when you add some additional elements to the adventure, the enjoyment level escalates.

FISHING

Fishing is an activity that almost anyone can participate in. Even small children can go fishing, but parents must supervise and assist at all times. It is a good idea to pinch the barb of the hook in if it will be used by small children. A pair of pliers will allow you to squeeze the barb down against the shaft of the hook. The child will still be able to catch fish, but if an accident does occur, you won't have a barbed hook stuck in your child. The puncture will still be painful, but you will be able to remove the hook with minimal trouble and damage.

Small children should be equipped with a life vest, even when fishing from shore. The child's curiosity or attempt to catch a frog might cause a fall into the water.

How much gear do you need to take your children fishing? A complete fishing outfit for a child can be purchased for less than $20. This gear will consist of a rod, reel, line, hooks, bobbers, and perhaps a tackle box. Bait can be worms, crickets, grasshoppers, marshmallows, bread, or about anything else you can think of.

There are all types of rods and reels available. There are even very short rods, made especially for little tykes. A closed-face spinning reel is the easiest to use. These reels only require a thumb on a lever and a toss at the water to operate. Due to their closed-face design, these reels don't foul the line like an open-faced reel.

Young kids won't care if they are fishing a blue-ribbon trout stream or a creek with hardly more than minnows in it. For kids, fishing is all the fun that is needed. The size and type of fish caught is not nearly as important as it would be for adults.

Fishing can provide some great campfire meals. What could be better than having fun and catching supper at the same time? However, before eating the fish you catch, be sure the waters the fish are taken from are not polluted. Fishing is fun, and it is an inexpensive addition to your camping activities.

HIKING

Some people would say spending the day walking up and down mountains is not fun; it's work, but many people do enjoy hiking. Hiking is good exercise and it goes together well with camping. Many people enjoy hiking so much that they take up backpacking. This allows them to set up camp in remote areas and enjoy the serenity of nature, away from vehicles and masses of other campers.

Strapping on a day pack and going for a walk in the woods is good for the soul. It is also good for kids. Children have a lot of energy to burn, and hiking is one way to ensure an early bedtime.

CANOEING

Canoes are a fine means of transportation for campers. Canoeing allows campers to reach wilderness areas without the strain of backpacking. Canoes are also excellent vehicles for fishing beaver ponds and other small bodies of water that might be difficult to access on foot.

Floating down a slow-moving stream can expose parts of nature you wouldn't see hiking. Ducks, deer and other wildlife won't run from a gliding canoe like they would from the crashing of hiking boots coming through the woods.

Canoes can be tricky to operate. Long canoes, about seventeen feet long, are much more stable than short canoes. If you decide to add a canoe to your camping equipment, get used to it before going into deep or fast water. Make sure your children are trained in how to keep a low center of gravity and to restrict movement in a canoe. It doesn't take a lot of action to tip a canoe. Personal flotation devices should be used on every trip.

As a part of your training, you should simulate what will happen if the canoe is flipped over in the water. This training should take place in shallow, still water, under controlled conditions. Teach your kids to grab onto the canoe if it flips. The canoe will help keep them afloat and will provide a means of rest for soggy floaters.

PHOTOGRAPHY

Taking a camera along on a camping trip is as natural as leaves on a tree. The extent of the camera equipment can vary from a $10 disposable camera to over $10,000 worth of professional gear.

Many parents overlook the possibilities of what small children can do with a camera. We let Afton use my expensive equipment with supervision, but she also has her own 35mm camera. The pictures that she takes with this camera are enough to make anyone sit up and take notice. There are many inexpensive cameras available. For most applications, a 35mm camera will be the best choice, but 110-format cameras will also give some good photos.

When a child goes out with a camera, you never know what will come back on the film. When the film is developed, you might find pictures of a tree, a bug, the sky or yourself. I develop a lot of my own film, and when I am developing and printing pictures that Afton has taken, I'm always excited to see what's on the roll. You and your child can enjoy this same excitement when you open the envelope and see your developed pictures for the first time.

BIRD-WATCHING

Bird-watching is a major-league activity for some people, and it is fun for all ages. A pair of binoculars or a spotting scope will make the adventure more exciting, but bird-watching doesn't require any expensive equipment. The naked eye is very efficient when it comes to watching birds. This type of activity can be kept as simple fun, or it can be developed into a learning process and a serious hobby.

ROCK COLLECTING

All kids like rock collecting. Normally, it is enough to fill pockets with rocks, but some children will want to take the activity to higher levels, which might include a formal collection of semiprecious stones. A rock tumbler is a big asset for serious collectors.

CRAFT PROJECTS

Craft projects are numerous and work well at the campsite. By taking a few basic items, like paper and glue, along on your trip, kids can use natural materials to make all kinds of projects.

Log Cabins

Log cabins, on a miniature scale, are easy to build at camp. Glue is the only material needed from home. Kids can collect twigs and branches off the forest floor. Once the collection is complete, the twigs and branches can be fashioned into a log cabin. The wood can be stacked and glue can be used to simulate the chinking done on real log cabins.

Once the shell is constructed, the roof structure is framed out of the same materials. When it is time for the roof covering, pine needles, leaves or moss can be used to cover the rafters. Doors can be made from fallen tree bark. The bark can also be used to simulate the shutters of pioneer cabins.

If you will be camping for an extended period of time, a complete fort can be constructed with similar techniques. The walls of the fort will be branches stuck into the ground. The buildings inside the fort will be built like the log cabin. This type of activity can consume hours of otherwise restless time for creative kids.

Acorn Necklace

An acorn necklace can be made with a piece of string and the caps from acorns. After punching a hole in the top of acorn caps, they can be strung onto the string. If you don't have any string, a vine can be substituted, but be sure it isn't a vine that will cause a skin irritation. Collecting the acorns is half the fun of this project, but the end result is a wilderness necklace.

Pinecone People

Pinecone people can be fun to make and can be used as toys or ornaments for a Christmas tree. Finding pinecones with just the right shapes will be fun, and transforming the pinecone into a doll or ornament is easy. Pine needles can be used for hair; it can be attached with clear glue. Twigs can be attached to represent arms and legs. Leaves can be used for clothing. Making these projects will be enjoyable, and the end result will be a toy to play with at camp and at home.

Wilderness Montage

A wilderness montage can be made in a way presentable for framing. You can use a piece of cardboard, burlap, or whatever as the background for the montage. Then, collecting and gluing various forest elements, like leaves, pine needles and bark, to the background will create a graphic interpretation of what is found in the woods.

Craft projects for the camp are limited only by a person's imagination. If you need help in coming up with viable projects, visit your local bookstore or library for books written on the subject.

TREASURE HUNTING

Treasure hunting is fun for kids of all ages, even grown-ups. The treasure sought might be gold, gems, old coins or seashells. All that is needed for this activity is a collecting bag to hold treasures that are found. Older kids and adults can add to the enjoyment with a metal detector.

Metal detectors for young children are available with prices of less than $50. More sophisticated versions can cost upward of $600. There are many variations between these two extremes.

Before setting off with your metal detector and digging tools, make sure the activity is not prohibited or restricted in the area you plan to explore. Also, be sure to keep digging to a minimum and cover all holes.

Panning for gold in streams is another way for all family members to seek treasure. Gold pans are not expensive, and most any type of pan can be used. There are still plenty of streams giving up gold to those who seek it.

If you want to rig the game, you can bury your own treasure for children to find. You might even draw a treasure map for the kids to follow in their search for buried treasure. This is great fun for the kids and a low-impact activity for parents.

There are, of course, many other options for adding fun to your camping trip. Many of the same activities enjoyed at home can be incorporated into camping adventures. The key is to spend a little time thinking about where you will be and what you would like to be doing.

Chapter Eight

HOW TO TURN RAINY DAY FROWNS INTO HAPPY SMILES

I can remember several times when I was relaxed by the rhythmic sound of the rain tapping on our tent. I would settle in and read a book or chat quietly with my spouse. But try to tell your kids to just lie quietly and listen to the rain. It will last for about two minutes, tops. When I was growing up, rainy camping days were to be expected. It seemed to rain often in late summer on the coast of Maine. Contrary to the quiet time my parents would have liked, all I wanted to do was go outside, stomp through puddles, and get drenched. The rain did not whisper to me to relax, it loudly called to me to come and play.

TURN ADVERSITY TO ADVANTAGE

There are many entertaining alternatives to just sitting together inside waiting for the rain to stop. Consider the various reactions your children will experience throughout the day. They will have energy to burn, disappointments to reconcile, and depending on your camping conditions, they may be physically uncomfortable. Be conscious of the changes in your children throughout the day and look for diversions that will alleviate each level of boredom or frustration.

Start the day with a simple breakfast, such as cereal, which is easy to make and eat, and quick to clean up. Then it's time to exercise your family's minds. Here are some interesting scientific facts and simple experiments for rainy days.

Molecules

Grab a bag of large marshmallows and a box of toothpicks, and open a can of peas or corn. Give your children a pile of each item and begin talking about what rain is. Rain is made of water. Water is made of small pieces called molecules. The scientific name for water is H$_2$O, which stands for two parts hydrogen and one part oxygen. Smaller children do not need to understand this concept in depth, just enough to see that water is made by joining two small parts of hydrogen to one large piece of oxygen. Now have your family put a toothpick in the top of the marshmallow and one off the left bottom edge. They then attach a kernel of corn or one of the peas to the toothpicks and they have created a model of H$_2$O.

Then you can let them play for a while making imaginary molecule models. Some kids will construct intricate building cubes and triangular structures with the materials. Anything that challenges their minds and keeps them entertained is fine.

An Inch of Rain

Children hear the weatherman say that you can expect an inch of rain to fall today, but how can they tell if it rained that much? Simple; give them each an empty can to put outside in an open area to catch the rain. The cans do not have to be the same shape or size. When your kids are ready to measure the rain, give them each the same size paper cup and have them pour their rainwater into the container.

Prompt them to see if they each have the same amount of water in the cups. You can give them a ruler or a stick to measure with. Ask what kind of factors could affect how much rain is in one can versus another. Did one have leaves or other materials fall into it that would displace the water? Talk about what displacement is and explain that objects in the water push it out of the way and raise the water level.

The crow and the water pail. Here is an old fable that explains water displacement very well. "Once there was a very thirsty crow who went looking for water. He spied a pail of water sitting next to a well and went to quench his thirst. To the crow's disappointment, the pail was too deep, and the water too shallow, for him to perch on the side of the bucket and get a drink. How could the crow get a drink?" Ask your children if they have any ideas about how the crow might solve the problem, then continue with the story.

"The crow hopped over to the gravel road, next to the well, and picked up a rock in his beak. He walked back to the pail of water and dropped it in. Back and forth the patient crow went, picking up rocks and pebbles and dropping them into the bucket. Finally, after quite some time, the crow hopped onto the side of the pail and was able to get his much awaited and greatly deserved drink." The rocks displaced the water until it was close enough to the top of the pail for the crow to drink.

Thunder and Lightning

If you are having a really big storm, your smaller children may become anxious about the scary lightning and the loud thunder. Understanding what makes the light and the noise and figuring out where the storm is often turns a frightening storm into a fascinating lesson. You can vary the sophistication of the explanation to meet the level of understanding of your children. Simply put, lightning is electricity. It is created when opposites bump into each other. You can give your youngster a wooden spoon and a metal one. The wooden spoon is made of positive pieces and the metal spoon is made of negative pieces. Let your child hit the spoons together a few times to simulate clouds colliding.

Clouds have these same positive and negative parts called ions. These are the same things that make magnets stick to metal. Rain clouds full of positive ions are pulled toward clouds of negative ions and they crash together. When they hit, they make electricity, like a big spark, that races away from the clouds through the sky. This is lightning.

As the lightning cuts through the air, it leaves a gap. Put the palms of your hands together and ask your child to push a hand between yours to separate them. Now clap your hands loudly together. That is the sound of the air crashing against itself as it fills in the gap left by the lightning — the sound of thunder. Toddlers will enjoy clapping their hands and shouting boom when the thunder sounds. For them, understanding the relationship between the clap and the sound of thunder is fulfillment enough.

Your other children will be interested to know that light is faster than sound. Your family can approximate how far away the storm is by watching the lightning. Once they see the flash, have them count the seconds until the sound of the thunder. It takes five seconds for the sound to travel a mile. You can do the math for younger children. Divide the seconds between the flash and the thunder by five to find the distance of the storm. Fifteen seconds from lightning to thunder, divided by five seconds per mile, means the storm is three miles away.

Mount Saint Sally

When your children seem ready to erupt with energy, have them build a volcano. This project is great because kids always seem to really get into designing and decorating the volcano. They can use homemade "playing dough" (there is a recipe on p. 97) or commercial clays and doughs. Have the children model the volcano in a large pan. Encourage everyone to adorn the mountain with twigs, sand, or other materials leftover from field trips and gathering expeditions. They need to cut off the bottom half of a paper cup and use it to form the opening at the top of the volcano. When the masterpiece is done, give each child one of the following ingredients to pour into the paper cup, in this order:

- ¼ cup of water
- 1 tablespoon of baking powder
- A squirt of red food coloring
- A few drops of dish detergent

The final ingredient is ¼ cup of vinegar. When this is added, the volcano will bubble over. Don't worry, there is no messy explosion. Your kids can repeat the eruption over and over as long as the ingredients hold out, and clean-up is easy.

INDIAN RAIN DANCE

Learning about rain and making volcano gods angry probably won't keep your kids busy all day. Eventually, their energy levels will rise and they will need to move. You will begin to see them become restless, their attention spans will diminish, and they will hear the rain calling to them to come out and play. This is an ideal time for you to make it rain yourself. This activity is best done in a camper or cabin, but if you're tent camping you can take the family out under the tent fly if you think you can keep them from jumping around in the wet.

All you need is a camp stove, a large pan of water, a smaller pan of ice cubes, and another cup of water. Heat the large pan of water to boiling. While you're doing this, have your kids make up a rain dance. The idea is to get them jumping, stomping and moving around. When the pan of water comes to a boil, ask the youngest child to pour a cup of cool water into the pan of ice cubes. Hold this pan over the boiling water. The steam from the boiling pot will begin to condense on the bottom of the pan of ice water. Before you know it, your little rain dancers will see it rain!

PITTER PATTER AND NOT MUCH CHATTER

After a quick lunch of sandwiches, sliced fruit, and vegetables, getting your family to take some quiet time should be relatively hassle-free. Encourage children to look through their nature books or to make a list of the items they would like to collect when the rain is over.

Look for ways for your family to calm down. Perhaps each child could pick a nature subject to write about. The topic could be what kinds of things live in the sea and how they move around. Do they have fins or flippers? Do they propel themselves or are they carried by the tide? You might suggest a list of various plants and the ways they defend themselves. Blackberries have thorns, skunkweed smells, milkweed tastes bad, and poison ivy itches. See how many senses your children can include in their observations or concentrate on just one.

Many younger children will be ready for a rest after this time-out. Older children may be content to research their subjects or read. A few hushed verses of "Rain, Rain Go Away," or similar gray-weather songs are always nice. This is also a good time for the adults to sit back and relax to the murmuring rain.

WHEN THE RAIN WON'T GO AWAY

At some point you may find yourself succumbing to the cries of restless children demanding to go outside and play in the rain. Often this can happen if you have had several days of rain and have depleted your arsenal of interesting ideas. It is difficult to stimulate a family that has cabin fever. Desperate times call for desperate measures, and you may have to break down and let the kids go outside.

However, the consequences for such a field trip are many. If you are tent camping you will need a trash bag for wet clothes, a container for muddy boots, and lots of towels and warm, dry clothes. Even RV and cabin campers must be prepared to minimize water infiltration into the living space caused by many pairs of dripping pants and grimy footwear. Be prepared to make a trip to the laundry facility with your bundles of drenched garments and sneakers to be dried.

You will be faced with these complications anyway, as your family makes trips through the rain to the bathhouse or car. We advocate packing old shoes and extra socks for just such an occasion.

When there is a gentle rain, nature puts on her delicate hat. Your family will see camp with a different perspective. Leaves and rocks glisten, raindrop prisms fill with color as they drop from branches, tree bark gets darker, and the smell of moss and humus fills the air. Sure, the kids get wet feet, but getting out and seeing this side of creation is far better than tying them to their seats and praying for sunshine. With rain, you must learn to go with the flow.

Chapter Nine

CAMPING AS AN EDUCATIONAL FIELD TRIP

The educational value of camping to your children cannot be over-looked. Nature is a wonderful teacher. Kids can explore the woods and fields to learn about life cycles and much more. Streams provide plenty of learning activities. Camping at different times of the year will expose your children to new sights and sounds. If you are willing to be creative, nature can teach your children many lessons.

MAKING A COLLECTION

Leaf Collecting

Leaf collecting is a good way to spend some time in the forest. Kids can find an abundance of fallen leaves on the forest floor. The leaves can be placed in collecting bags or between the pages of a notebook for transportation back to camp.

Once the leaves have been taken into camp, it will be time to identify each leaf. With the help of any of the many resource picture books available on plant identification, finding the origin of the leaves will be fairly simple.

When a leaf is identified, it can be glued or taped to a piece of paper with its name written below it. In addition to the name, a brief description of the leaf and its tree can be specified. Then, the sheet of paper can be placed in a three-ring binder as a part of a leaf collection.

This is a fun activity for children, and it teaches them about trees and leaves. The learning process is enhanced by the research involved in identifying the leaves. Children learn to use resource materials to answer their questions. This type of learning will come in handy at school.

As a variation of leaf collecting, kids can collect berries, nuts, and other items dropped by plants and trees. Building a comprehensive collection of leaves, berries and nuts can take several trips to accomplish. Therefore, each time you take your kids camping to different spots or during different times of the year, their collections can grow. This is a nearly endless activity.

Finding Fossils

Finding fossils can be fun and easy. By looking around streams, lakes, ponds and rock outcroppings, fossils can be turned up. Many of the fossils may go unnoticed to casual campers, but ardent investigators can find them.

Once fossils are found, they can be the beginning of yet another type of collection. Studying the imprints of fossils will lead to curiosity, and the curiosity will lead to further investigation in history books.

Rock Hunting

Rock hunting can be educational, as well as entertaining. In fact, you never know when your kids will turn up a semiprecious gem. Even if finding gemstones is not the major motivation, rock hunting can provide hours of recreation.

As rocks are found, they can be stored in collecting bags. After the bags are full, some time with reference books will allow your child to identify the various rocks. If you invest in a rock tumbler (they can be had for under $50), your child can make jewelry from the rocks collected.

Beachcombing

Beachcombing is not only fun and relaxing, it can be very rewarding. A stroll along the beach can turn up numerous types of shells and other collectibles. By studying shells, children can learn about the countless creatures in the sea. Collecting shells is fun and can be done in about the same way as leaf collecting.

ANIMAL OBSERVATION

Animal observation is a broad term that may encompass a variety of activities. Good binoculars will help with these activities. Bird-watching is perhaps the best-known means of animal observation, but it is by no means the only one.

A whitetail deer (fawn)

Pulling a Net Through a Stream

Pulling a net through a stream can yield unlimited learning opportunities. The net might catch tadpoles, fish, snakes, snails, plants, eels, or any number of other watery mysteries. Since not all catches will be desirable, like some snakes and leeches, teach your children to be careful of what they touch.

As the net is brought to shore, children can inventory their catch. To avoid hurting the stream's inhabitants, don't keep them out of water for long. Have your children look through the contents of the net and jot down their findings. These streamside notes can become a part of a growing library of environmental facts for your kids.

Casting Animal Tracks

Finding and casting animal tracks can be interesting and educational. When tracks are found, they can be filled with a casting material, such as plaster of paris (found in arts and crafts stores). When the plaster is dry, it can be removed as an impression of the track.

Casting animal tracks is easy and the molded tracks can make a conversational collection. Matching the tracks to the animals that made them is a good way to learn about animals. In researching what types of animals made the tracks, kids are sure to learn other fascinating facts. Afton loves to cast moose tracks.

DISCOVERY LOGS

Discovery logs serve many purposes. These logs can be compiled to create some interesting historical data, or they may contain a list of animal tracks that are found, a record of weather conditions, or just about anything else.

A discovery log can be a pocket-size spiral notebook or individual sheets of paper that will be stored in a loose-leaf binder. A child's imagination is the only limitation on discovery logs.

Children can take barometric readings and temperature readings to record in their logs. They can note how many crows they saw on a particular day and when and where the crows were spotted. Directions to semisecret places can be kept in a discovery log. Children can spend hours making entries in their journals.

CLOUD FORMATIONS

Cloud formations can be mesmerizing. Have you ever lain on your back and watched the clouds go by? Did you ever imagine what the shapes of the clouds resembled? Do you know the difference between a cirrus and a cumulus cloud? Observing clouds provides plenty of opportunity for youngsters to stay busy.

When a kid combines cloud watching with a discovery log, the results can be impressive. Children can lie on their backs and let their imaginations run wild. Clouds can resemble animals, ships, fruits and much more.

Studying scientific cloud facts is not only educational, it is a part of your children's survival training. Knowing what types of clouds indicate threatening weather can save their lives, or at the least make them more comfortable.

There is a side benefit to watching clouds. While lying on your back, you see the whole world from a different perspective. You might see hawks riding thermal currents or squirrels dancing in the treetops.

Fluffy Dandelions

Blowing on fluffy dandelions can be fun for anyone. However, watching the downy fluff fly into the air is also educational. When you take the time to explain to your children how the fluff disperses seeds, they will learn how plants continue their existence.

THE BIRTH AND DEATH OF A TREE

The birth and death of a tree can be an interesting project to study. It can start with the little helicopter-type seed pods most kids love to throw in the air. The life cycle of a tree is pretty easy to document. You can show your children an acorn on the ground. In the next step, point out an acorn that has begun to sprout and take root. Then, finding a seedling that is beginning its stretch for the sky will supply another piece of the puzzle. The next move is to find a sapling and then a full-grown tree. Follow this step in locating a dead or dying tree, and then a fallen tree. The final piece of the puzzle is examining a decomposing log that is returning to a mass of humus.

Putting the complete puzzle together may require multiple out-ings, but each find can be recorded in the discovery log. This type of search-and-study mission should hold the attention of your chil-dren and make for a fine educational experience.

THE MICROSTRUCTURE

The microstructure of a forest holds many interesting sights. It is a forest within a forest. Have you ever studied an old tree stump that is covered in moss and fungus? If you have, you know how many living things can be found in the tiny space of a tree stump. This is a microstructure, and microstructures are amazing.

Even as an adult, I spend a substantial amount of time exploring a single microstructure. If I'm out with my camera and macro gear, I look for microstructures. There is never a doubt in my mind that these little worlds will hold dozens of potential pictures.

While your children may not be looking for photo opportunities, microstructures assure them of some engrossing scenes. A magnify-ing glass will add to the discoveries possible under these conditions. Give a kid a reference book, a magnifying glass, a discovery log, and some time around a microstructure, and you should have a contented child.

BUG BINGO

Bug bingo is a game children can compete in. Parents can make bingo cards that have pictures of bugs on them. When the cards are passed out to the children, the game begins. Each child ventures out to find the bugs on the card. Parents can act as referees when bugs are found. The bug-bingo cards are marked to indicate discoveries. Playing by normal bingo rules, the game is played until one child has a bingo. If you want the game to take awhile, have the kids play blackout bingo, where every bug on the card must be found. Not only will this game consume considerable time, it will teach kids how to identify various bugs.

SCAVENGER HUNTS

Scavenger hunts have been enjoyed by children for years. As a creative parent, you can send your kids on some educational scavenger hunts. For younger children, the targeted treasures could be a rock, a pinecone or leaf. For older children, the list of items to be found can be more complicated, such as an oak leaf, a granite stone or the needle of a white pine tree.

Kids will enjoy the competition of scavenger hunts, and they will be learning at the same time. This is a good way to hold children's attention while at the same time teaching survival skills. By making a scavenger list of edible wild foods, you can train your children to find and identify lifesaving natural foods.

FROM EGGS COME FROGS

A learning project that is fun involves discovering that from eggs come frogs. A walk around a pond is likely to reveal the jelly-like bunches of frog eggs that cling near the edges. Observations of the eggs over a period of time will show that they produce tadpoles. Further investigation will prove that tadpoles turn into frogs.

While watching frog eggs turn into frogs is difficult in the wild due to the time between stages, it is easy at home. By collecting a small sample of frog eggs in a container filled with water from the pond, you can transport them home. Once the eggs are placed in an aquarium filled with pond water, children can observe the changes that occur.

If you decide to pursue this project, it is important to place a screened top on the aquarium. It is equally important to provide structure in the aquarium that will allow the frogs to get above the water level. In the tadpole stage, water is enough, but as the tadpoles change into frogs, they will need resting places that offer air to breathe.

Learning From the Mistakes of Others

Learning from the mistakes of others is a good way to teach your children camping etiquette. When you are out camping and see where others have abused the environment, point it out to your children. Tell them what has happened, the effect it will have on our world, and why it shouldn't be done.

Examples of these misdoings could include litter, trees that have had their bark peeled off (like the birch trees in Maine), ruts cut into the earth by off-road vehicles, and the like. By showing children what not to do, you are ensuring a better future for new generations.

SCULPTING WITH SNOW

Sculpting with snow is always fun. Who doesn't enjoy building a snowman from time to time? Well, snow can be sculpted into many shapes, and this type of activity will bring out the artist in your children. Don't limit snow projects to building forts and making snowballs and snowmen. Encourage your children to be creative. Let them build snow castles. They do it in the sand, why not do it in the snow? Help your children build statues of wildlife with snow.

When the children get interested in building lifelike snow sculptures, they will spend time thinking about what to construct. Research might be conducted to get the statue just right. Then, when the snow is manipulated into a sculpture, it will have special meaning, and the children will be proud of their accomplishments.

TRACING NATURE

Tracing nature is a good way to learn and to build a scrapbook of nature. All that is needed for this activity is some paper and a pencil. Putting the paper on a textured surface, like a rock or tree bark, and rubbing the pencil over the paper will produce interesting designs. Most parents have done this type of thing with coins, but tracing nature offers many more opportunities.

The tracings can be used to create a game, which can be played among children or with an individual child and parents. After numerous items have been traced, use the drawings to play a guessing game. The child that did the tracing can pass the paper around to other game contestants. Each contestant can guess at what the tracing is. The first person to guess correctly wins a point. Then, if there is more than one child playing, another child can pass a tracing around.

The limits of nature's educational value is set only by people's creative levels. Some people will sit in the woods and think there is nothing to do; others will kneel by a microstructure for hours, observing what many campers never notice. As a parent, you can make trips into the out-of-doors both fun and educational.

Chapter Ten

CAMPING TIPS FOR CHILDREN OF ALL AGES

This chapter is chock-full of tips and tidbits for more enjoyable camping. We will share with you advice to keep you from making the mistakes we've made during our many years of camping. These tips will help you in any type of camping.

Special provisions are necessary when camping with small children. Infants require even more specialized gear. Fortunately, there is plenty of equipment available to make camping and hiking with infants possible.

There are many types of backpacks and child carriers for active parents. Collapsible cribs and playpens are a near necessity for infants and toddlers. Strollers allow more freedom for parents when the terrain is such that a stroller can be used, and wheeling kids around reduces back strain. There are many types of pack-along equipment that can ease the burden of parents in the field.

Special care must be taken when children are in a new environment. Whether the new place is a friend's home, a playground or a campsite, kids need to be aware of the changes in their surroundings. This is especially true when kids are being introduced to camping for the first time.

Special care is needed not only for preschoolers but for all inexperienced campers. As a parent, it is your responsibility to educate and advise your children about the dangers and benefits of camping.

Should You Take a Gun?

Should you take a gun for protection on your wilderness camping trips? This is a tough question, but the generic answer would have to be no. The risk of the dangerous situation that demands a gun is far less than the risk of an accidental discharge where parents or children could be harmed.

Take a Lockable Container Along

Parents with young children should, when feasible, take a lockable container along. This container can be used to house dangerous fuels, matches and other objects you don't want the kids to get into.

Do an Auto Check

You should do an auto check before venturing into the wilds. A weak battery or a rotted hose can leave you and your family stranded in the wilderness. Taking care of your vehicle should always be a consideration, but when you will be driving into rough backcountry, these checkups are even more necessary.

Take a Variety of Clothing

Take a variety of clothing with you on camping trips. The weather can change quickly. Any major shift in weather conditions can cause the clothes you left the house in to be unsatisfactory.

Don't Overdress the Kids

Don't overdress the kids. Dress children in layers of clothing and monitor them closely. If they are getting too hot, remove a layer of clothing. If you allow your children to work up too much of a sweat, cold temperatures might use the perspiration to fuel hypothermia. In hot weather, keep an eye open for heat exhaustion.

Beware of Cold Water

Parents must beware of cold water. Mountain streams can run cold, even in the summer. A child's body is not as stable as an adult's. Letting kids splash in shallow streams can be great summer fun, but hypothermia can strike even in relatively warm temperatures.

Thin Ice

Thin ice takes the lives of many people. Don't take chances with ice-covered water. Ice skating is fun, but it should never be done on ice above deep water.

Bright Colors

When camping, dress your kids in bright colors. Clothing that is easy to spot will make keeping up with roaming children much easier. It will also help protect them from hunters.

Shoes Required

Shoes should be required for kids wanting to wade in water. There is no way to know what is at the bottom of a stream, puddle or pond. Glass, sharp rocks, sharp seashells and other dangerous things can hurt the feet of the ones you love.

While shoes should be required for wading, hip boots and baggy waders should not be worn by children. If a person falls into the water with chest waders or hip boots on, the footgear can fill with water and drown the wearer.

Mark a Boundary

Mark a boundary at your campsite. The boundary can be marked with surveyor's tape or visual landmarks, but kids should have a limit on how far they can go without adult supervision. This tip will help reduce the risk of a lost child.

Old Boots

Old boots are better than new boots on hikes. If you buy new boots, break them in before taking them on the trail. Wearing comfortable footwear will minimize blisters.

Whistles

Whistles are fun to play with, and they work well for calling dogs, but they are also good for finding misplaced children. Give your children whistles to carry with them at all times. If a child becomes turned around in the woods, a quick blow on the whistle can signal you as to the child's whereabouts.

Books

Books are great for camping trips. Small children will enjoy picture books. Teenagers will know what they want to take in the way of reading material. Game books can be fun for the whole family. And who knows, you might need the paper to get your fire started, if you haven't mastered your outdoor skills!

Hats

Hats should be packed for all campers, especially babies. A baby's head is especially vulnerable to the sun's rays. Hats also give biting bugs a place to land, other than your head. Many bugs will land on the highest point available. Would you prefer to have mosquitos on your head or on your hat?

Protect Their Faces

If you take your children camping in cold weather, it is important to protect their faces. This point is especially important when the wind is blowing. We all know about wind-chill factors, but we don't always take the precautions we should. The skin on a child's face is sensitive and should not be subjected to prolonged exposure during cold days. Applying petroleum jelly to the face or having the child wear a full-face stocking cap can help to protect tender skin.

In warm weather, sun tan lotion or a good sun-blocking lotion should be a part of your gear. You need to protect the tender skin of children from both hot and cold situations.

Pillows

Pillows are often forgotten on camping trips. Extra clothing can be bundled up to act as a pillow, but real pillows make sleeping much more pleasant.

Weather Reports

Never depend on weather reports. Always go prepared for the best and the worst weather you are likely to encounter. A decision not to take rain gear because of a forecast of clear skies can result in a lot of time trapped inside your tent or RV. With the proper rain gear, you and your kids can get out of your confinement, even if only for a short time.

Cull the Crop

Cull the crop of your camping gear. By keeping notes of the equipment you do and don't use, you can lighten your load on subsequent camping trips.

Blowing Bubbles

Blowing bubbles can be fun for kids and therapeutic for adults. A small bottle of bubble fixings is not much to carry, and it can provide a lot of fun.

Pack Safely

Pack your load safely. Never pack your vehicle in a way that the load might shift and hurt passengers if the brakes are applied quickly or the car is struck in an accident. Use a checklist to avoid forgetting wanted items.

Favorite Stuff

Don't forget your child's favorite stuff. Some children can't deal with not having their favorite blanket, toy or pillow. There may be nothing worse than spending a camping trip with a child deprived of a favorite possession.

Plastic Bags

Plastic bags can be a big help when camping with kids of all ages. The bags can be used to store soiled diapers and wet clothing. A makeshift rain poncho can be fashioned out of a large trash bag by cutting holes in it for the head and arms. Smaller, reclosable bags come in handy for keeping collectibles safe for the return trip home. Just remember, don't leave the plastic bags where a child could get one and suffocate. These bags should be packed in the lockable container we previously recommended.

Don't Overlook Natural Activities

Don't overlook natural activities when you are camping with your kids. A lot of parents fail to recognize all the opportunities that exist in the outdoors as natural entertainment.

We have gone camping when families in the vicinity were equipped with more electronic gear than we have at home. Hand-held video games, televisions and VCRs packed in with the camping gear are not unusual equipment for some campers. If you get too caught up in commercial entertainment and convenience, much of the charm of camping can be lost.

Make a Sundial

Are your children constantly asking you what time it is? Get them interested in answering the question for themselves with a sundial. Each child can make a sundial and personalize it with markers, stickers, leaves, moss or shells. A simple sundial can be made from two large paper plates.

Cut one plate into a square. Next, bring opposing corners of the square together and fold into a triangle. The triangle will have two short sides and one long side. Mark a center point on the remaining paper plate. Stand the triangle upright on the paper plate at the center point and attach with tape, staples or glue. Use a compass to find magnetic north and position the sundial on the ground or table so the long triangular edge points north. Each hour have your children mark the location of the shadow cast by the triangle onto the paper plate and write the time at the mark. After several hours, they will be able to measure between the time marks and manually complete the hour locations. Then your children will be the proud owners of a clock with no moving parts, and they won't ask you the time every five minutes.

Enjoy Your Surroundings

Teach your children to be observant and to learn from their surroundings. Bring magnifying glasses, small bug containers and collecting bags. Your kids can create a homemade magnifying glass out of a paper cup. Poke a small hole in the bottom of the cup and put the cup against your eye. Look down through the cup and out of the small hole. Things look larger than before.

The secret is that the small hole cuts down on the amount of light that enters your eye. The concentrated light waves make objects appear larger than normal.

Encourage your family to think about the life around them. If you are in the woods, look for a tree stump and show your kids how to tell what kind of life the tree had. Count the number of rings in the stump. Each ring represents a year of the tree's life. Wide rings indicate the tree had a good growing season, thinner rings represent hard winters and poor growth. Ask your kids to think of what kinds of things could affect a tree's growth.

Look at living trees and observe their shape. What could cause a tree trunk to twist or bow out? Does it look like the tree has lost many branches? Talk about what could cause these changes. Soon your family will be forming a hypothesis and making up stories of hungry porcupines and burly lumberjacks.

Listening Skills

Did you know you can tell the temperature by listening to a cricket? Have you ever heard a squirrel bark? Are you aware that crows and bluejays will warn their wilderness neighbors that you have invaded the forest, long before you finish setting up camp? You won't have to tell your kids to keep it quiet if you teach them such interesting facts. They will spend their time tiptoeing around, trying to keep leaves from rustling and twigs from snapping so they can sneak up on bugs and animals.

Birdcalls and bird-watching can provide hours of pleasure. Even young children can imitate a cardinal or a chickadee. Old and young alike will enjoy finding birds in books and reading about their habitat and habits. You can look for woodpecker holes while you are evaluating the life cycle of trees and see how they tie together.

Specimens

Your children can capture bugs in fields and streams and try to find out what kinds of animals and fish eat them. They can trace the life cycle of a creature and plot its place in the food chain.

Everyone can take a collecting bag and gather leaves, moss, rocks and pinecones for examination and speculation back at camp. Once my cousin and I spent all day collecting rocks along the Colorado River. The next day was spent assembling them into a model of the Rockies. No one had to keep us entertained or stimulate our imaginations. We just observed and enjoyed our surroundings.

Keep It Safe and Simple

Keep these tips in mind on your next outing and you're sure to have a more enjoyable camping experience. Consider safety and comfort as well as education and entertainment. Most of all, get out there with your kids and look at ants, listen to crickets and wade through streams. You will rediscover a childlike wonder and appreciation.

Chapter Eleven

CAMPFIRE COOKERY

Campfire cookery is not only fun, but it offers an opportunity to create some delicious dishes on an open fire. Though some areas restrict or prohibit the use of open fires, many places don't. Nearly every organized campground will provide fire rings to contain your campfire. In the wilderness, you can build your own fireplace without much trouble. In fact, building the fireplace can be almost as much fun as watching, smelling, and cooking with the fire.

FIREPLACE MATERIALS
How you go about building your fireplace will be determined by the materials you have available. Let's start our discovery of fireplace construction with the materials you might work with.

Rocks
Rocks are what the majority of wilderness campfire containers are made from. Rocks for a fireplace should be dry. Wet rocks, like those found in or along a stream, can be dangerous. As the fire and rocks get hot, the moisture in the rocks will turn to steam. The force of the steam is enough to explode the rocks, sending rock slivers and chunks flying through the air.

Even rocks that are pulled from the ground can contain enough moisture to cause problems. If you have any doubts about the moisture content of your rocks, stand clear of the first fire you build. After the rocks have been through a complete cycle of a hot fire, they should be dry enough not to worry about in subsequent fires.

Logs
Logs can be used to fashion a fireplace. The primary purpose of the fireplace is to contain the fire and to block any wind that may whip the fire out of control. While logs will burn if they are too close to the fire, they can still be used effectively by digging a fire pit. Once

the pit is dug, the logs can surround the pit, blocking wind and still being out of reach of the flames and intense heat.

Dirt

Dirt can be an effective barrier against wind. When you dig your fire pit, you are going to have some dirt to put somewhere; you might as well surround the pit with the dirt. The same could be done with sand. In most areas you are going to have either sand, dirt or rocks underfoot, and any of these will serve to protect your fire pit.

FIREPLACE CONSTRUCTION

Fireplace construction is an activity that the whole family can participate in, and it's fun. If you will be using rocks, you can send the kids out on a collecting mission. This gives the youngsters something to do, as well as a sense of pride in the project, and it saves your back from bending so often.

While the rocks are being collected, someone can begin excavating the fire pit. This part of the job is not as much fun, but it is a necessary element of a successful fire. The fire pit should have a diameter of between two and three feet. A depth of twelve inches is enough for any cooking fire. However, if your rock walls will not be high, you might want to dig the pit a little deeper. Keep the dirt that is removed from the hole close by. You will need it to refill the hole, and you might need it as an emergency fire extinguisher.

Once the collection crew returns with the rocks, have them stack the rocks around the fire pit. Flat rocks work best, but all rocks can be used if the stonemasons take their time and use some ingenuity. Once the rocks are in place, you're ready for firewood.

In our trips through the mountains, we have come across some impressive fireplaces. Some were complete with chimneys and multiple cooking levels. We've even gotten carried away with the enjoyment of stacking rocks and made some exotic fireplaces of our own. However, a simple round fire ring is all you need.

KEYHOLE COOKING

Keyhole cooking is one of the best ways to perform your culinary duties at camp. A round fireplace is okay for cooking, but a keyhole

A keyhole fireplace

fireplace is great! This type of fireplace allows the most flexibility in your cooking and produces the best results.

A keyhole fireplace is, unsurprisingly, made in the shape of a keyhole. There is a large semicircle at one end that is connected by a narrow cooking strip to a small semicircle at the other end (see photo above).

In this type of fireplace, the large semicircle is where the fire is built. As the fire produces hot coals, the coals are raked away from the flames and placed in the cooking strip. The fire pit for the big semicircle is about a foot deep and the cooking strip has a depth of about six inches.

Hot coals produce a much more even heat than flames. This makes cooking much easier and the results more consistent. By having the coals in the cooking strip, you don't have the high heat of the main fire cooking you while you're cooking dinner. When you get serious about campfire cookery, you must experiment with a keyhole fireplace.

PREPARING THE FIRE

Preparing the fire correctly is an essential step in cooking with a campfire. There is more to gourmet camp cooking than sticking a pan over a blazing flame. Start building the fire with small wood. As the fire starts to burn, add more wood, but not big logs. Branches will be better than larger pieces. Your goal is to develop a hot bed of coals as quickly as possible.

As the fire continues to burn, feed it more branches. When the flames turn from yellow to blue, you are getting a hot fire. Soon, you should see the unmistakable glow of red embers. Once you have an adequate pile of red or white coals, you are ready to cook. It is okay to let the flames die down; the coals will stay hot for hours.

DEALING WITH WET WOOD

Dealing with wet wood can be frustrating when trying to build a fire. Inexperienced campers often go without a fire because of wet weather. It is not that these campers want a cold camp, they just don't know how to build a fire when they only see wet materials around them. To keep you from having such unpleasant experiences, we're going to show you how to find dry tinder, even in the wettest conditions.

Tree Bark

Tree bark on dead wood can save the day when you want a fire after a hard rain. Cut bark off of fallen trees (dead wood only, please). The inner bark is likely to be dry. When this bark is shredded with a knife, it makes excellent tinder. Once you have a couple handfuls of tinder, you can stack the rest of the dry inner bark, in tepee style, over the tinder. One match should be all it takes to get this type of tinder going.

Hollow Trees

Hollow trees can hold a wealth of dry, burnable material. Many dead trees collect dry leaves in their trunks. However, be careful retrieving these dry goods. You never know what might be living in the leaves.

Under Uprooted Trees

When big trees with large root structures fall to the forest floor, they act as a roof to a small section of the forest. The root ball holds one end of the tree off the ground. The angled position of the tree allows the creative camper to find dry tinder and kindling beneath it.

Under Stream Banks

Look under stream banks for a collection of dry materials. Overhanging stream banks are often clogged with leaves and branches. These materials are deposited by wind and high water. Most people wouldn't look near water for dry fire goods, but it is an excellent place to hunt for tinder and kindling.

Second-Layer Findings

Second-layer findings can save the day. If you are camping in a mature forest, the depth of the forest floor can be deep. Even when the first layer of the forest floor is soaked, digging a little deeper may reveal some dry goods.

Cheating

Cheating can be okay. If you have reason to believe you will run up against wet woods, you can cheat and take tinder with you. Packing a little dry tinder won't get you expelled from the school of camping. If anything, you should get a merit badge for going prepared.

IT'S AN ART

Campfire cooking is an art. It is one thing to warm a cup of instant coffee over an open flame or cook a marshmallow, but it is quite another thing to produce pizzas, surf-and-turf dishes and casseroles over glowing coals.

Cooking with children can be rewarding and enjoyable for everyone. Camp cooking provides the challenge of preparing appetizing menus with minimal ingredients. Combine camping and cooking with kids, and you have the opportunity to create masterful menus that are both fun and delicious.

As a child I was introduced to camp cooking by my mother during our annual trips to Maine. The first lesson I learned was never to

Cooking a marshmallow over a campfire

count on the weather to cooperate with your menu plans. Many times my mother stood under a tarp cooking dinner in the rain. When I grew older and began fending for myself at the campfire, I purchased many books on cooking outdoors. I was amazed at the complex, gourmet meals that required hours to prepare. From those frustrated experiences came my own discovery that the key to successful camping is meals that are quick and easy. This lesson is particularly significant when you are preparing meals with your children. No longer will you be hounded by the incessant question, "When will dinner be ready?"

You will need the basic tools of the trade. While nonstick pans are fine for propane stoves, they may not tolerate overheating from an open fire. Also, the plastic handles on steel pans can start to melt from the intense heat of coals. If you will be cooking on a fire with your children, I recommend bringing several cast iron skillets with lids, elbow-length oven mitts, a fire grate and a long-handled spatula. When using a fire grate, I often bring the grate from our barbecue grill and position it on rocks over the coals of my keyhole fire pit.

My mother always had a camping box stocked with standard ingredients such as salt, pepper, premixed seasonings, flour, oil and sugar; I strongly urge you to do the same. Always include jars with lids, plastic bags, a whisk and a potato masher. You will be surprised at the pleasure your little ones will take in crushing fruit for shakes and spreads and mashing and smashing potatoes, and winning pudding-shaking contests.

Plan for a kid's night when you give your children a selection of ingredients and allow them to make their own imaginative meals. This idea is particularly successful with the recipes I have included for Petite Pizzas and Kid's Casserole (both on p. 92). If you involve your children in the preparation of food and keep the cooking time to a minimum, everyone will be enjoying meals more.

My strongest recommendation is that you measure all of the ingredients in separate containers for your children to combine. You can prepare parts of the meal while your children are mixing the rest. Kids love to sift, stir and whip, and it can keep them busy for quite a while.

Prepared foods can provide you with a short-cut to success. I often bring boxed pizza mixes, instant skillet dinners, and pancake mix which only require that you add water.

I believe in breakfasts that are fast and nutritious. Instant oatmeal, French toast, and scrambled eggs are always on my list. If you choose to indulge in omelettes or bacon and eggs, fix the main course yourself. There is no easy way for children to cook these foods, with hot grease splattering and eggs quickly overcooking. Instead, ask your helpers to garnish the breakfast plates with slices of banana or oranges. Earthquake Shakes (see recipe on p. 94) will complement any breakfast and keep the kids busy for as long as necessary. My family doesn't like to spend a lot of time at the breakfast table when surrounded by nature, and I prefer not to waste much time afterwards cleaning pots and pans. We usually take the quick path through the morning meal.

Our lunch menus vary, depending on the day's activities and weather. Try to avoid routine sandwiches and chips, and include high energy foods at noon. Fruits and vegetables make excellent side dishes at lunch, especially when served with Double Dip (recipe on p. 94) on the side. One of our favorites, Super Sloppy Joes (p. 93), is quick and easy enough for children to make themselves. If your little campers present you with a stringer full of fish, fry them in bread crumbs while the kids make tartar sauce (p. 91) and Watergate Salad (p. 93). When rain or cold ruin your picnic plans, try Pop Pop's Slumgullion (p. 91). This hearty soup cooks up in about fifteen to twenty minutes and is very easy. All you do is put it on the fire and play cards until it's done. No-fuss lunches can be full of nutrients, fast, and fun, come rain or shine.

Dinnertime gives you the chance to prepare fabulous feasts with the help of your children. When the fire makes you think of supper on a stick, consider Porcupines (p. 93). These simple kabobs are made with ham and pineapple, and are guaranteed to make your mouth water as they cook over the flames. If you plan to grill hamburgers or cook spaghetti for dinner, put your helpers to work on dessert. Fill a large jar with instant chocolate pudding mix and two cups of milk. Close the jar tightly and let your kids go crazy shaking it. By the time the burgers are done, dessert will be ready too.

If making plain pudding doesn't keep your youngsters occupied long enough, move to plan B. Give them a box of graham crackers to demolish. Once the crackers have become crumbs, measure out 1½ cups and add ¼ cup of sugar and ½ cup of melted butter. When the children have combined the ingredients, they are ready to press the mixture into a pie pan. Now give them a second jar full of powdered dairy whip and milk. Once this round of shaking is over, they can mix the pudding and dairy whip together in a large bowl. Spoon this mixture into the piecrust, and you have chocolate mousse pie — complete with kids who will be calm (if not darn right pooped) all through dinner.

The recipes that follow encourage children's participation by combining simple ingredients and easy preparation. I've left out the stew that takes two hours to cook and the campfire Beef Burgundy. In their place, you will find the makings of meals that will have everyone smiling and asking for more.

FUN FRIED FISH

1 egg
Juice of 1 lemon
½ cup flour
8 slices of bread
Seasoning
3 tablespoons oil
Fish pieces

Lightly toast bread in skillet. Children should then rub each piece of toast between their hands or rub across a cheese grater to grind into crumbs. Place bread crumbs, flour and seasonings in plastic bag. Mix egg and lemon in a bowl and dip fish pieces in mixture. Put fish in bread crumb bag and shake until completely coated. Fry fish on skin side for 5 minutes. Turn and cook additional 5 minutes or until fish flakes easily.

TWO-SECOND TARTAR SAUCE

1 cup lite mayonnaise
1 teaspoon minced onions
3 tablespoons sweet pickle relish

Combine all ingredients.

AFTON'S AWESOME APPLES

2 apples per person
1 tablespoon margarine
½ teaspoon cinnamon
1 teaspoon sugar

Peel and slice apples and put in a plastic bag. Add cinnamon and sugar and shake to coat. Melt margarine in skillet and warm apples for 3 to 5 minutes or until soft. This recipe is listed on a per person portion.

Tip: The thinner you slice the apples, the more quickly they will cook.

POP POP'S SLUMGULLION

1 can corned beef
1 onion
8 medium potatoes
Salt and pepper to taste

Peel and dice potatoes, and chop onions. Place in 4-quart pot and fill half the pot with water. Bring to a boil, and add corned beef—broken into small chunks. Salt and pepper to taste. Reduce to a simmer by lowering flame or thinning coals. Cook for about 20 minutes. Serves 4.

KID'S CASSEROLE

1 can drained tuna
1 can cream of mushroom soup
1 can peas
1 box macaroni and cheese
¼ cup water
¼ cup margarine
Topping (see Note)

Boil macaroni as directed. Combine cheese sauce mix, ¼ cup water, ¼ cup margarine, mushroom soup, and peas. Mix in macaroni. Pour mixture into skillet and heat for 5 minutes. Cover with topping before serving. Serves 4.

Note: Topping possibilities include 1 cup crushed crackers, 1 cup smashed saltines, or 1 cup broken potato chips (the assorted pieces at the bottom of the bag).

Tip: If your children don't like tuna, substitute a can of chicken a la king.

PAN PIZZA PIE

1 box pizza mix
½ cup mozzarella cheese
2 tablespoons margarine
Toppings

Mix pizza dough. Omit adding any oil. Melt 1 tablespoon of margarine in skillet and remove from heat. Coat hands with margarine and gently stretch dough. Press dough to edges of skillet and heat for 2 minutes over hot coals or medium-high heat. Remove from heat and spread ¼ cup of sauce over crust. Sprinkle cheese on pizza and add toppings such as pepperoni, onions, mushrooms or cooked sausage. Cover skillet and cook pizza for about 2 minutes or until cheese melts completely.

PETITE PIZZAS

4 English muffins
1 can spaghetti sauce with meat
4 slices mozzarella cheese
Additional ingredients as desired

Spread spaghetti sauce on each half of the English muffins and top with slice of mozzarella cheese. Place in a skillet, cover and heat for 3 minutes—until cheese melts.

Tip: Children are limited only by their imaginations when adding additional ingredients. Some suggestions include: pepperoni, olives, sausage, and vegetables.

EASY-TO-DO BBQ

1 lb. ground beef
1 tablespoon sugar or honey
1 cup catsup
1 tablespoon mustard
1 teaspoon Worcestershire sauce
1 tablespoon vinegar

Brown hamburger in skillet. Add other ingredients and heat 5 minutes. Serve on hamburger buns. Serves 4.

PORCUPINES

1 can chopped ham
1 can pineapple chunks
1 green pepper

Cut ham and green pepper into 1-inch cubes. Drain pineapple chunks. Alternate green pepper, ham, and pineapple on skewers or sticks. Cook over fire 2 to 3 minutes.

SUPER SLOPPY JOES

1 can corned beef
¾ cup catsup
1 each onion, green pepper, stalk of celery

Melt 2 tablespoons of margarine in skillet. Add vegetables and cook until soft (about 5 minutes). Have children break corned beef into chunks and mash until fine. Add corned beef and catsup to vegetables and simmer for 5 minutes. Serve on hamburger buns. Makes 8.

WATERGATE SALAD

1 box powdered dairy whip
1 can crushed pineapple, drained
1 box instant pistachio pudding mix
1 cup miniature marshmallows

Mix dairy whip by adding milk and shaking in a jar. Mix pistachio pudding mix in another jar. Pour contents of each jar over crushed pineapple in a large bowl. Add marshmallows and toss together.

SIMPLE SCRAMBLED EGGS

8 eggs
½ cup milk
Salt and pepper to taste

Beat eggs thoroughly and mix in milk, salt and pepper. Melt 2 tablespoons of margarine in frying pan, and add egg mixture. Cook, stirring frequently until stiff. Serves 4.

Note: Kids really enjoy stirring scrambled eggs. The key to success is cool coals, which allow slow cooking. Try adding 3 slices of cheese for a tasty variation.

FAST FRENCH TOAST

2 eggs
¾ cup milk
6 to 8 slices white bread
3 tablespoons sugar
¼ teaspoon nutmeg or cinnamon

Beat together eggs, milk and nutmeg. Melt about a tablespoon of margarine in the skillet. Dip each piece of bread in the egg mixture and coat well. Fry each side until lightly brown. Serve with syrup. Serves 3.

EARTHQUAKE SHAKES

2 cups cold water
2 tablespoons honey
½ cup nonfat dry milk
1 large can peaches

Mash peaches and pour into a jar. Add honey and water, sprinkle in dry milk and shake well. Serves 4.

DOUBLE DIP

¾ cup sliced carrots
8 oz. low-fat plain yogurt
1 oz. orange juice
¼ cup water

Boil carrots in water until soft. Drain off water and mash carrots to a pulp. Add yogurt and orange juice, and mix thoroughly. Goes well with fresh fruit or vegetables.

FANCY FRUIT SPREAD

Fruit as listed*
½ cup sugar
¼ cup water

Arm cooks with potato mashers, and have them turn the fruit into pulp. Add water and sugar and warm in a skillet about 2 minutes, stirring often. Serve warm or cool on toast. Makes about 6 ounces.

Apple spread: Use 6 to 8 medium apples, dice before mashing, and add 1 tablespoon of cinnamon.

Peach spread: Use one large can of peaches.

Grape spread: Use about ¾ pound of seedless grapes.

S'MORES

2 large graham crackers, broken into 4 pieces
1 plain chocolate bar
2 marshmallows

Break chocolate bar in half. Toast marshmallows. Put half the chocolate bar on a graham cracker, top with hot marshmallow, and cover with another graham cracker. Repeat with remaining chocolate, marshmallow and cracker.

FISH CHOWDER

2 cups cooked fish
1 can cooked potatoes
2 onions, chopped
1 quart whole milk
½ pound bacon or salt pork
2 tablespoons margarine
Salt and pepper to taste

Slice salt pork into ¼-inch cubes and fry. If using bacon, fry and break cooled pieces into chips. Cook onions in drippings until clear, drain. In a large pot, add all ingredients and heat thoroughly for about 10 minutes. Stir often and be sure *not* to boil. Serve with crackers.

Tip: This recipe can be used for oyster chowder and clam chowder as well.

PASTY POCKETS

Pastry Ingredients:
4 cups flour
1½ teaspoons salt
1 cup margarine or shortening
2 ounces water

Filling:
1 lb. ground hamburger
1 medium can sliced potatoes
1 medium onion
Salt and pepper to taste

Have children mix all pastry ingredients and divide into four parts. Roll out dough on floured surface to 8 inches in diameter. While kids make the pastry, cook onion in melted margarine until soft, about 5 minutes. Brown hamburger and drain off grease. Drain potatoes. Toss hamburger, potatoes and onion together in a bowl. Place equal amounts of mixture in the center of each pastry. Fold edges to cover filling, dampen fingers and seal crust into a pocket. Fry pockets on each side in melted margarine until crisp.

Tip: You can substitute leftovers such as steak, barbecue, and baked potatoes. Vary recipe by using sliced pepperoni and a slice of cheese in each pocket.

Note: This dish was a favorite of Welsh coal miners, providing them with a hearty alternative to sandwiches. The term "pasty" is more well-known in certain northern climates, such as New England, northern Michigan, and so on.

GRIZZLY STEW

1 jar peanut butter
10-pound bag potatoes
1 bear
2 rabbits (optional)

Open jar of peanut butter as bait to trap bear. Kill and clean bear and cut into small cubes. (This will keep the kids busy for about 2 days.) Peel potatoes and cut into 1-inch cubes. (Add another 6 hours to preparation time for the children to complete this.) Fill 50-quart kettle half full with water. Brown bear meat and add meat and potatoes to water. Simmer for 3 days. (Children will have ample time to make bearskin rugs.) Serves 30 people. If more than 30 people arrive, add 2 rabbits for extra meat, but exercise caution—some people don't like hare in their stew.

Tip: Have fun with all the recipes; add to them, and try substitutes. Sometimes the best recipe is no recipe at all. Roughing it encourages children to try some unorthodox combinations which can become family favorites.

PLAYING DOUGH

1 cup of flour
½ cup of salt
1 cup of water
2 teaspoons of cream of tartar
Food coloring

Combine all dry ingredients in a large saucepan. Add water and stir with a wooden spoon or stick over medium heat. Keep stirring. The mixture will start off runny and then will quickly stick together. When the mixture thickens, remove it from the heat and stir into a ball. Flip the ball of dough onto a floured surface and divide into smaller balls. Put each ball into a bowl and have your children add different food colorings to each ball. Knead color into dough as it cools. Store in airtight plastic bags.

Chapter Twelve

GETTING THROUGH THE NIGHT

After a day of collecting bugs, explaining nature, and running to keep up with your inquisitive kids, you will probably be ready to collapse in your sleeping bag and fall fast asleep. Don't be surprised, however, if your children are not ready to follow your lead. Be prepared to provide adequate wind-down time for your happy campers to ensure that you all get a good night's sleep.

GATHER AROUND THE FIRE

Some of my favorite camping memories are of times our family sat around the campfire toasting marshmallows, singing songs, and telling stories about Great-Grandma Wagner or the time Dad caught the big fish. These were relaxing moments when we would all cuddle together and watch the flames perform their hypnotic dance. Sometimes my brothers would fall asleep and have to be carried to their sleeping bags. Time by the fire can do more to get your kids ready for a peaceful sleep then any amount of coaxing or demanding.

The purpose of this time is to provide an opportunity for your children to relax. Sleeping away from home can be difficult for kids. Even teenagers, well accustomed to the friendly sleepover, can have problems sleeping when camping. The bedding is a different size and firmness than they are accustomed to, they may get hot or cold easily, and there are a lot of unusual noises to contend with.

One of my worst memories of a night in the woods was when I went camping with a teen group. We were fourteen years old, on average, and we built a big bonfire down by the beach. There we sat, all snuggled up under blankets, when our chaperon began to tell us ghost stories. At the end of one particularly suspenseful tale, he jumped up with a yell and threw dry seaweed into the flames, which crackled and popped like firecrackers. I went to my tent anything but relaxed! All night I heard strange noises, saw shadows move past my tent, and lay in my bag with wide eyes and pounding heart until morning.

Quiet time before sleep is not always enough. Even without ghost stories, many children become overtired, overstimulated, or over-anxious about sleeping out. Here are a few of the bedtime games we play before sleep.

DO YOU HEAR WHAT I HEAR?

As adults, we learn to block out the background noise we are sub-jected to daily. Children don't do this, and many times they are concerned about sounds you never heard. Do you hear what I hear is a way to acclimate children to the night sounds of camp. You start by saying, "Do you hear what I hear?" Your child will immedi-ately stop stalling or wiggling and listen. Then you proceed. "I hear a small chirping sound. What do you think it could be?" Your child will strain to hear the sound and will either respond that he or she hears nothing or give a suggestion of what is making the sound.

If your child doesn't hear the noise, ask what kinds of noises he or she does hear. If your child hears a sound, begin to talk quietly about what the animal might be saying, such as, "I think the cricket is saying good-night to the forest. He is yawning and saying, 'Good-night tall, cool grass. Good-night bright shining stars. Good-night warm, soft leaves.' "

Speak in a relaxing manner about sleepy things and your child will begin to unwind. Sometimes really excited children will tell you the animal is calling all the other animals together for a party or it is telling the nighttime animals to wake up and get moving. At this point, pick another sound, like the gentle breeze blowing, and con-tinue.

SHADOW BUNNIES

Most of us have made hand shadows on the wall and thought it was great fun. Our daughter, Afton, is frightened by shadows and gets concerned about dark shapes that move across the tent wall. We start our sleeping ritual with hand shadows. First we have fun mak-ing as many shapes and sizes of shadows that the flashlight and our hands and feet will generate. After several minutes of giggling and guessing what the shadow is, we begin the good-night-shadow game.

I turn off the light and say, "Good-night shadows." Then, if Afton spots any tree shadows on the tent wall she will point out the stubborn silhouette. I turn on the flashlight and tell the shadow that it must go to sleep. Shining the light on the tent makes the shadow temporarily disappear. Of course, when I turn the light off, the shadow returns. Then I ask Afton what shape the shadow is making. Prompted by our hand-shadow game, she will say it is a duck or dog or turtle. Then I tell the animal that I will let it stay in the tent so long as it watches over Afton through the night or goes to sleep. In this way the shadows become friendly things that don't startle her should she wake up in the night and see them.

STAR LIGHT, STAR BRIGHT

Older family members may enjoy star gazing as a way to relax and prepare for sleep. Everyone can enjoy finding and identifying constellations. Most people are familiar with the Big Dipper, the Little Dipper and the North Star. With a star chart and some patience, you can find many more interesting formations in the night sky. Astronomy is enticing and entertaining. Toddlers love to find the wishing star and make a good-night wish.

Twinkle, Twinkle, Little Star

Can your family tell the difference between a star and a planet? While they have their eyes fixed on the heavens, tell them to see which lights are twinkling and which seem to cast a constant light. Stars are farther away than planets. Since stars radiate over great distances, their light is broken up and appears to twinkle. Planets are closer and shine with even intensity.

On a clear night, your teenagers might even be able to see a satellite. As they watch the sky, your kids might see small lights that shine brightly like planets but which move through space. A satellite's movement can be tracked by the naked eye. A telescope enhances the ability to find and follow satellites. Your children can create a makeshift telescope out of a paper towel tube. The large opening at the end of the tube allows more light in the eye and makes things look larger.

COMFORT FIRST

Children may be tired and ready for bed, but feel uneasy and unable to sleep because of their environment. Smaller children are particularly susceptible to temperatures, shadows, noises and even smells. The backyard trial run we suggested in chapter two may have gone off without a hitch, but suddenly your four-year-old can't sleep in a campground. This may be because in the trial run the child was close enough to home and all the associated security not to be worried. Now the same child won't let you turn off the lantern and leave the tent.

I recommend that you prepare your child for sleep when you first set up camp. Make sure your son has his flashlight next to his pillow. Show your daughter how to unzip the sleeping bag and tent and how to find you if she wakes up in the night. Make certain everyone knows how to get to the restroom or how to use the portable toilet and that they have toilet paper available.

NIGHT LIGHT

Provide fluorescent strips along the walls of your camper or RV that lead to the bathroom, and be sure that your young children know how to get out of their bunk beds or cots so they don't feel stranded or helpless. Also, don't give children much to drink before bed. This minimizes the need for them to get up in the night. Making your children comfortable with their sleeping quarters and surroundings will make it easier for them to get to sleep. Glow-in-the-dark toys can make the dark less intimidating for younger children.

TOO HOT, TOO COLD, JUST RIGHT

Temperatures may vary dramatically during the night. When my family camped in Maine during summer vacations, the temperature swings were striking. You could come home from a warm day on the beach only to change into sweatshirts and long pants for dinner. I hated going to bed in a sleeping bag. I'm one of those people who likes to move around a lot, and the confines of a sleeping bag made it impossible for me to get comfortable. I would finally get to sleep only to wake up several hours later, burning hot. After wrestling with the zipper, which always stuck, I would surface from my prison to cool down. I would barely have time to fall back asleep before I began to freeze!

These memories haunted me as I looked for ways to protect our daughter from the night air while providing her with the opportunity for blissful slumber. The answer was a sheet between Afton and her air mattress and a layer of covers. A flannel sheet, an open sleeping bag, and a spare blanket have met every changing climate we have camped in.

LOUD NEIGHBORS

Despite all your good preparations, your children's sleep may be interrupted by neighboring campers. Late arrivals, group gatherings, and cookouts can affect your kid's rest. Once our daughter could not get to sleep because neighboring campers had made a bonfire. The flames were so bright that our tent was lit up like the midday sun. I ended up putting a towel over Afton's eyes to block out the light and she fell asleep quickly.

There have been times when we had to ask noisy neighbors to lower their clamor to a reasonable level so we could sleep. It may surprise you that one man's whisper is another man's scream. On one occasion, I asked the campers across the road to turn down their radio. They looked at me in disbelief and complained that they could barely hear it as it was! Seeing a no-win situation emerging, I had to think fast. I had noticed earlier that they were from Virginia and decided to solve the problem in a cordial manner. I invited them over to our site for coffee and dessert and to talk about our old home state. The night proceeded nicely and our daughter slept like a baby. If this had not worked, I was prepared to go to the owner of the campground. Most organized campgrounds have a quiet time and a lights-out rule. Ask about such rules and procedures when you check in.

THINGS THAT GO BUMP IN THE NIGHT

At this point, let's assume that you were able to relax your children with a flickering fire and soothing songs. They are comfortable, tucked into bed, and are sleeping soundly. The neighbors have all turned in, and the forest has settled into its quiet nocturnal rhythm. What do you possibly have to worry about until morning? How about tapping at the windows, midnight snacks, and creatures banging on your head?

The best laid plans can be thrown out the window by Mother Nature. This is what separates camping from staying in a motel. It's the adventurous part, the thrill of the great outdoors, the unexpected that will bind your family together with a fabric of wonderful memories.

When I was young, we traded our pop-up for a hardtop camper. The first night we had a cloudburst. Rain bounced off the roof like falling Ping-Pong balls. Everyone woke up in confusion, and after we pinpointed the source of the racket, we had a good laugh and went back to sleep. Another night, the wind blew tree branches against the side of our trailer, and we thought someone was trying to get in.

BEARS AND OTHER BEASTIES

Then there was the time that a mother bear came into the campsite next to us with her twins. First she threw folding chairs around and made enough noise to wake up the entire forest. Then she sat down on top of the picnic table and proceeded to crack open our neighbor's cooler like a raw egg. It was quite a sight, and it took us all some time to relax enough to go back to sleep after the bear family left.

ENJOY THE EVENING

Several times during encounters with the unknown, I have found that, as the adult, I was more concerned than the kids around me. Afton was able to sleep through a thunderstorm one night while I lay waiting for the tent to collapse. Other times, concepts which seemed ordinary to me were fascinating to children. Once we stayed in a campground that my family had frequented when I was young. I knew from experience that raccoons launched nightly raids on the campsite trash cans. Not wanting Afton to be frightened by the inevitable commotion, I calmly explained the possible evening's encounter.

I should remind you at this point that earlier I stressed that the goal of bedtime rituals is to relax your children. Well, my explanation backfired. Afton was so excited about the idea of watching raccoons tear into our trash that I needed an hour to get her ready for sleep again.

Remember, camping is a time to be together as a family. It should be fun, entertaining and educational. I've found it best, sometimes, to keep my concerns and even my well-intended explanation to myself. Let your children provide questions about their concerns or discomfort. There is no need to guess if the neighbors are disturbing them, your children will make enough ruckus about not being able to sleep because of the noise. If you educate your children about nature, and provide a safe, comfortable camping environment for them, everyone can have an enjoyable time and a good night's sleep.

Chapter Thirteen

GETTING GEARED UP

Getting geared up for affordable family fun is fun in itself. Planning what you want, how you will use it, and where you will get it can be almost as much fun as using it afield. However, the gear needed for camping with children may be a little different than what you used for adults-only camping. This chapter will give you the knowledge to avoid frustration and capitalize on enjoyment when choosing your camping gear.

TENTS

Tents are usually the first type of home away from home that new campers experience. Many seasoned campers never go beyond this type of simple protection from the elements. Why do so many people depend on thin nylon to keep them dry and warm? It's because tents are effective, light in weight, and relatively inexpensive.

Cabin Tents

Cabin tents are ideal for family camping. It is possible to buy a cabin tent that is divided into separate rooms, and this is always helpful when camping with kids. What makes cabin tents so good? They offer plenty of headroom, and due to their design, cabin tents have tall walls that offer substantial space for sleeping and playing. Having the extensive area of a cabin tent will be much appreciated if you and your children are forced to weather out a storm in the tent.

Dome Tents

Dome tents normally provide adequate space in a stable tent that is easy to set up. Once domes are set in place, they generally remain stationary. These tents are great for most any camping occasion, and since they almost set themselves up, they are particularly good for the single parent with a child along on the trip.

Modified-dome tent without a rainfly

Modified-Dome Tents

Modified-dome tents (see photo above) are similar in style, features, weight and price to dome tents. While appearance of these tents may differ from true domes, the concept is about the same, and modified domes often have a little extra room in them.

SLEEPING BAGS

Sleeping bags are an important part of every camper's equipment. A good sleeping bag will keep you comfortable in a wide range of temperatures. Let's examine the different types of sleeping bags and what you should look for when shopping for quality and comfort.

Designer Bags

When young children are a part of your camping plans, you will unquestionably become aware of the many designer bags available. These sleeping bags are decorated with colorful characters that all children can identify with. The bright colors and friendly faces make these bags appealing to small children; however, the functional aspects of these sleeping bags leave something to be desired.

Designer bags are usually not meant for use in cold weather. If you plan to spend the night outdoors on any but the mildest of evenings, these bags will not provide adequate warmth for your children. For summer camping and slumber parties, designer bags are fine, but don't look to them for serious camping in cold weather.

Mummy Bags

Mummy bags are well known for their shape and ability to make the most of body heat. These tapered sleeping bags are designed to provide tight sleeping quarters. By keeping the bag small and tapered, it retains body heat better. The disadvantage to these efficient bags is their lack of room to move around. Children may feel confined and uncomfortable in a mummy bag.

If you are buying sleeping bags in a store, try them on for size, literally. Have your kids crawl into the bags and check the fit. Depending upon the size of your children, you may want to investigate bags made in smaller sizes. A small child sleeping in an adult-size bag will not receive the maximum benefits of comfort in cold temperatures.

Rectangular Bags

Rectangular bags provide more room for movement than mummy bags do. While rectangular bags may not be quite as efficient as mummy bags, the additional room gained from the design is usually worth the trade-off.

Rectangular bags often have soft, cuddly liners. These liners may be made of flannel, cotton, or some other type of material. The soft linings add a feeling of warmth to the bag, and in some cases, the liners are designed to increase the cold-weather comfort zone. The cozy lining is a big asset for children who need a little extra comfort and cuddling to get to sleep.

SLEEPING FOUNDATIONS

Sleeping foundations increase camping comfort. The days of making a soft bed from leaves and pine needles are all but gone. Today, campers rely on foam cushions and air beds to give them a soft place to sleep.

Sleeping on Air

Sleeping on air is a preference of many campers. Air mattresses provide soft comfort and are good insulators between you and the ground. Some sleeping bags are made to accept an air mattress in a built-in pocket. The built-in pocket assures that the air mattress will remain under the sleeping bag, even if your children are active in their sleep.

When you shop for an air bed, look for quality. Good air beds have strong sidewalls and numerous interior supports. The supports should be vertical coils, not horizontal tubes. It is highly desirable to get an air bed that is covered on one side with an anti-slip material. It is no fun sliding across a slick air mattress all night when you are camped on a slight incline.

When you are camping with kids and dogs, air mattresses can get punctured. Make sure you take a patch kit with you for each mattress. The two biggest drawbacks to air mattresses are their susceptibility to ruptures and the need to inflate them.

Foam Pads

Foam pads are an alternative to air beds. They are lightweight, don't require inflation, and are not slippery. You don't have to worry about your child jumping on foam and poking holes in it.

Combination Foam and Air Mattresses

Combination foam and air mattresses are becoming available. These units contain foam, but they also self-inflate with air. All you have to do is open the air valves and the mattresses will take on the air they need. Some of these beds are equipped with integral pillows.

Cots

Cots offer an alternative to sleeping close to the ground, but they are not nearly as portable as pads and air beds. There is also a risk that a child might tip a cot over or roll off of it.

COOKSTOVES

Even if you plan to do all of your cooking over open fires, cookstoves are mighty handy on wet days. Also, not all locations will allow the use of open fires; when camping in these areas, stoves are essential to having warm food.

Camping cookstoves can be as simple as a folding piece of metal and a container of canned heat or as full-featured as you want them. The stoves can be fueled by canned heat, propane gas, liquid stove fuel, or unleaded gasoline just like you use in your car.

Propane Stoves

Propane stoves are probably the most popular type of campsite cookstove (see photo below). These stoves are fueled with propane gas. The gas is available in small, disposable cylinders that are easy to store and pack. Unlike a liquid fuel, propane is not messy, and you don't have to worry about the container turning over while transporting it. Additionally, you don't have to be concerned about your child drinking it.

Unleaded Gasoline and Liquid-Fuel Stoves

Unleaded gasoline and liquid-fuel stoves are another possibility for the campsite cook. These stoves are rated to cost less to operate

Propane stove

than propane stoves. Either type of heating unit will be more than adequate for cooking around the camp.

Personally, we favor the propane style. We don't like having to worry about our daughter getting into gas cans, and we don't like sloshing fuel all over our truck on rough roads. We feel safer with propane.

Cooking Accessories

Cooking accessories are helpful in the camp. The list of possible cooking accessories is a long one. If your cooking tends to get on the exotic side, you can have a Dutch oven for open-fire camping. A tripod grill will allow you to cook your food and heat your coffee at the same time. If you take some time to look through camping stores and mail-order catalogs, you can find every kind of cooking accessory you are likely to ever want.

LIGHTS

Lights are something every camp should have. Flashlights will be needed for some uses and lanterns will be desirable for other needs. There are many possibilities to choose from when it comes to lighting. The safest lighting to use when there are kids in camp is battery-powered lights.

Battery-Powered Lanterns

Battery-powered lanterns are not generally as powerful as gas-fired lanterns, but they offer many advantages. Since these lanterns don't use fire for illumination, you remove the risk of starting an unwanted fire. You also eliminate the possibility of your children being burned by a hot lantern. Unlike lanterns using potentially explosive fuel, battery-powered lanterns are relatively safe, and they can be used inside a tent.

Flashlights

Flashlights are always needed around camp. You should invest in at least one good flashlight and have a few other cheapies available for backup. Always go prepared with extra batteries.

PACKS AND BAGS

Packs and bags are usually a part of every camper's arsenal. You can purchase backpacks that are large enough to take provisions for weeks, and you can get little ditty bags for your personal affects. There are many packs available to fit children and dogs.

Basic Gear Bags

Basic gear bags are all most campers need. There is nothing fancy about these packs, but they get the job done. Gear bags usually have two handles and a shoulder strap. The bags are normally constructed of soft, water-resistant material. The sizes for gear bags vary greatly.

Basic gear bags are fine, but they don't hold a lot of stuff. We use a few gear bags, but we depend on duffle bags to transport most of our supplies and equipment. The large size and flexibility of duffle bags suit our needs best.

Day Packs

Day packs have shoulder straps and are carried on one's back. These packs will carry enough provisions for a day on the trail, but their capacities are limited, and day packs are not comfortable during long hikes.

Fanny Packs

Fanny packs are good for toting small quantities of supplies, but you won't get much in them. Some fanny packs have only one cargo pocket, while other models have three pockets. These lightweight packs are comfortable and handy. Each of us has our own fanny pack, and they see a lot of use on our camping trips.

Backpacks

Backpacks are ideal if you will be walking into camp. However, if you are a car camper, there will be little need for a backpack. You might, however, find a backpack made for carrying children very useful. It is never easy carrying a child along a trail, but a good backpack that is designed for the purpose will make the chore more manageable.

HEATERS

Heaters are an often wanted, but rarely practical, piece of equipment for campers. Most camp-style heaters depend on a flame for producing heat. Putting a flame-operated device into a tent is asking for trouble. The tent material, while often flame-retardant, is not fireproof. Another risk to putting a flame-operated unit in a tent is asphyxiation. Since oxygen is needed to keep the flame burning, the fresh air in a poorly ventilated area is quickly consumed.

There is also the risk of a small child coming into contact with a hot heater and getting burned. If you don't feel you can go camping without a heater, investigate the possibility of getting an RV that is equipped with a furnace or take up cabin camping.

TOILET FACILITIES

What camper doesn't consider toilet facilities? Well, never fear, equipment suppliers will be happy to provide you with portable toilet facilities, for a price.

Simplicity

There is something to be said for simplicity. Our favorite portable toilet is so simple that it is almost too good to be true. It consists of a lightweight, folding aluminum frame, a snap-on toilet seat, a

Folding portable
toilet

Bucket-style portable toilet

plastic bag, and a plastic retainer ring (see photo p. 112). This unit sells for about twelve dollars and is very compact. It can be a bit of a challenge for small children, however. Since a child's legs are not very long, the youngster may have trouble using this type of potty without tipping it over.

Bucket-Style Toilets
Bucket-style toilets (see photo above) take up a lot of cargo space and are famous for their owner's dislike in cleaning them. These units are about the size of a five-gallon bucket. The top of the bucket is molded into the shape of a toilet seat, and the units have snap-on tops. This type of portable toilet ranks low on our list of desired equipment.

Top-of-the-Line Toilets
Top-of-the-line toilets will set you back at least $80. However, if you don't want to have to dispose of soiled plastic bags, these units are your best option. These toilets have hidden storage

areas and are made to control odors.

If you feel the need for a privacy stall to take care of your natural needs, you can get one for about $25. Yes, you can buy the equivalent of outhouse walls to surround your portable potty. These privacy stalls consist of an aluminum frame and walls that resemble tarps. If you are camping in a populated area with a group of children, the privacy of this type of stall can mean a lot to everyone.

TABLES

Tables make a camping experience more enjoyable, and there are plenty of types to choose from. There are, however, three types of tables that are best suited to camping.

Roll-Up Tables

Roll-up tables take up very little cargo space and cost less than $35. This type of table will roll up into a package that is 32 inches long and has about a 5½-inch diameter.

Folding Tables

Folding tables (see photo p. 115) are our favorite. These tables provide plenty of surface area on a secure base, without taking up a lot of storage space. Additionally, the height of the tables is usually adjustable to accommodate up to four different height requirements.

Folding Picnic Tables

Folding picnic tables are a natural choice for parents that are sharing the campsite with their children. These tables provide seating for four and a surface-area dimension of about 34" × 53".

Seating Possibilities

Seating arrangements are a necessary consideration for campers. Seats can be fashioned from logs, stumps, folding stools and similar items. There are even seats that roll up into compact packages.

WATER CONTAINERS

We like water containers that collapse when not in use and that hold about five gallons when they are filled (see photo p. 116). These jugs are inexpensive and convenient.

Folding table

WATER PURIFICATION

Water purification is an important need for all campers who don't have ready access to potable water. Most family campers can carry a sufficient amount of drinking water in containers, but if you are walking into a remote campsite, carrying water will be no fun. For these occasions, you must determine how you will turn available water into safe drinking water.

Filters

Filters are an effective, but expensive, way to treat water. There are several options available for filtering water. For $45 you can have a portable water filter that will purify a quart of water in less than two minutes. For $125 you can get a portable filter that will produce a quart of water in about one minute. Some of these filters screen water for Giardia, coliform, salmonella, shigella, and other bacteria that can cause dysentery.

Filters are considered one of the best ways to conveniently cleanse drinking water, but they do have their disadvantages. Filters are famous for clogging and becoming useless. Some filters are frag-

Collapsible water jugs

ile and break on the trail. The cost of filters is prohibitive to many campers. Not all filters remove all risks from wild water. Before you buy a water filter, check it out closely.

Tablets

Most camping stores sell tablets to purify water. Tablets are not foolproof, but they are light in weight, inexpensive, and normally effective. Most purification tablets will take between twenty and sixty minutes to do their work effectively. If nothing else, these tablets should be carried as a backup water purifier.

Boiling

Boiling water is about the safest way to make sure it is safe to drink. High temperatures are very effective in killing bacteria. When boiling water, bring the water to a rolling boil and keep it there for between five minutes and fifteen minutes. In high altitude you will have to boil the water longer. While it may not be pleasurable to drink good, warm water, it is better than drinking cold, bad water. Remember not to let small children near the boiling water.

TOOLS

The tools needed for a successful outing depend on the type of camping you do, but there are some basic tools that most any camper will appreciate from time to time.

Knives

Knives serve many purposes in camp. Most campers will benefit from having two knives, not counting culinary blades. The first camp knife should be a multipurpose knife. These knives contain many useful tools, such as: scissors, blades, can openers, screwdrivers, awls, minisaws and corkscrews.

The second knife should be a sturdy, long-blade knife. A six-inch blade is plenty. This type of knife can be used as a digging tool, a personal defense weapon, a makeshift hatchet, and much more.

Shovels

Shovels are handy for digging fire pits and burying waste. While you probably will not want to take a full-size shovel to camp, you will

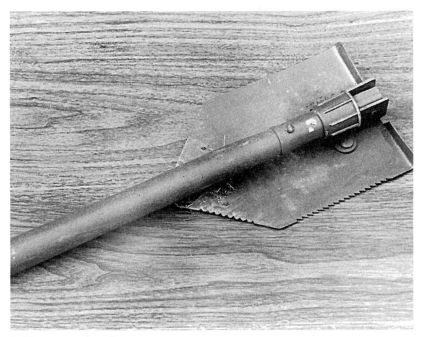

Folding camp shovel

enjoy the benefits of a folding shovel (see photo p. 117). This tool can act as a hoe, a shovel, and in a pinch, something of a saw. For less than ten dollars, you can include a folding utility shovel in your equipment inventory.

Axes, Hatchets and Mauls

Axes, hatchets and mauls are depicted as invaluable camping items, but in reality, there is not much need for them. A good saw will do a much better job of cutting firewood. A maul or a hatchet can come in handy for splitting wood or driving tent stakes, but you must be careful to protect your children from the sharp edges of these tools.

Saws

Whether you are making a lean-to or cutting firewood, a good saw will be much appreciated. Bucksaws are the most practical saws for campers (see photo below). They use replaceable, sharp, broad-toothed blades that make quick work of cutting wood with small to medium diameters. These saws come in various sizes. A small saw

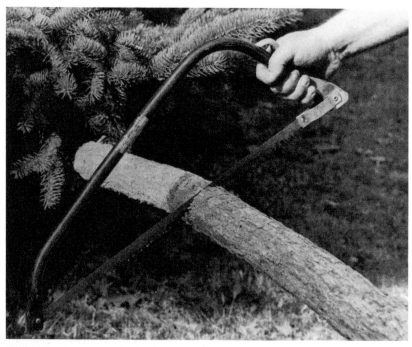

Bucksaw

with about a twelve-inch blade will handle most in-camp needs. With this type of saw, the shorter the blade, the sturdier the saw. However, if you will be cutting wood with a large diameter, you should consider a larger saw, say a 24- or 30-inch version. Please, don't cut down live trees; there is usually an abundance of dead-wood in the forest.

Chapter Fourteen

CABIN CAMPING

Cabin camping can be an ideal alternative to roughing it under a nylon roof or living in the cramped quarters of a small RV. In fact, cabin camping may be the best way to introduce young children to the wonderful world of camping.

We have stayed in cabins that have ranged from little more than a roof over our heads to shelters that would make some homes seem primitive. Some of the cabins have not been equipped with running water, bathrooms or electricity. Others had ornate stonework, beautiful fireplaces, modern appliances, central heat, electricity and more. As different as the various types of cabins have been, all have had enjoyable benefits.

Before we had Afton, we preferred wilderness cabins that gave us the feeling of being isolated. The thought of needing quick medical care and creature comforts was not of much concern to us. We knew that a call on the two-way radio would bring help by float plane or helicopter, and we just didn't worry much about anything unfortunate happening.

After bringing Afton into this world, our views changed. Being fifteen miles into the wilderness on an old logging road didn't seem like such a good idea. The thought of having to depend on an airlift to the hospital seemed irresponsible, and we shied away from some of our most favored wilderness haunts. This is when we started our civilized camping in cabins.

The first close-in cabin we rented was something of a disappointment. It was too close to the road (we could see and hear cars going by); adjacent cabins were inhabited by high-spirited fishermen; the community area was clogged with noisy, unsupervised children; and walks down nature trails where the frequent foot traffic had beaten a path an ATV could travel was not much fun.

After our first bad experience with cabin camping, we wondered if it would be different in other locations. The thought that all civilized camping would be equally unpleasant stuck in our minds.

However, we decided not to give up on cabins.

Our second experience with campsite cabins was totally different. The cabin had all the amenities a camper could want, but it wasn't tainted by the same problems we had experienced in the last cabin. There was a large lake behind the cabin and instead of listening to the screams of teenagers playing basketball, we were relaxed by the call of loons. Other cabins were close by, but the residents were quiet, and the setting offered a taste of the wilderness. Inside the cabin we had a kitchen, a fireplace, two bedrooms (another plus when camping with kids), a bathroom, and a lot of room to move around in.

As time has passed, we have become somewhat addicted to cabin camping. Afton is now old enough that we don't fear tent camping with her, but we all enjoy the comfort and security of the cabins. It is still nice to pitch a tent under a warm summer sky full of stars, but the cabins extend what would normally be a short camping season in the cold climate of Maine.

We have found that the trick to happiness with cabin camping is finding the right cabin in the right place. Through trial and error, we have built up a large inventory of potential camping sites that we know will not disappoint us. Now we would like to share with you our experiences and suggestions for cabin camping.

MAKE A LIST

One of the first steps to take before embarking on cabin camping is to make a list of all the amenities that are important to you. For example, if your kids can't live without television, make sure the cabin is equipped with electricity. Do you require a private bathroom, or will a public restroom within the camping area be satisfactory? Are you opposed to using a private outhouse? There may not be a lot of places left that use outhouse facilities, but in remote areas, like northern Maine, outhouses are still used on a large scale.

As you make your list, be sure to think through your camping time and try to plot a reasonable course of action. This will help you avoid missing important items on your list. The task is easiest if you start with your arrival and follow your intended activities to the time of departure. Here's a quick example.

Assume you will be cabin camping for the weekend with a small

A typical camping cabin

child. You will arrive at the cabin and unpack the vehicle. While you are unpacking, your spouse will have to keep an eye on your child. A deep-water lake abutting the cabin could be dangerous. A cabin with frontage on the main campground road would not be as desirable as one set back off the road with a driveway. The more distance you have between moving cars and your child, the better off you are.

Kids tend to enjoy running around without their shoes. They also seem to spend a lot of time on their hands and knees. A cabin with a rough wood floor might produce splinters that would harm your child.

As nice as a wood stove can be for warmth and atmosphere, the stove is a definite danger for a young child. Wall-mounted heaters are common in cabins. These heaters provide plenty of warmth, but they too can present a burn hazard for small children. A cabin with central heat will provide a safer environment.

If you will be camping during times of the year when heat and humidity are a problem, you may want to inquire about air-conditioning provisions. Not all cabins are equipped with air-conditioning, but many are.

A cabin with two bedrooms will be more enjoyable than a one-bedroom cabin. Some cabins have their sleeping quarters in lofts. While this is fine for older children and most adults, it provides another possible danger for a young child. If you will be using a cabin with a loft, make sure it has a solid safety railing and that there is a barrier between your child and the opening for the ladder.

There is also the question of bed linens. Are you required to bring your own, or are they provided? If you are camping with a very small child, a crib may be needed. Should you bring a fold-down crib, or will the owner of the cabin provide a crib upon request?

You will have to prepare meals while on your trip. Is the cabin equipped with a refrigerator and cooking facilities? Are pots, pans, dishes, glasses and eating utensils included in the rental? They are generally supplied with the cabins, but it is wise to ask before you go.

Once you have played out your stay in your mind, you will know what questions to ask when you are inquiring about the rental of a cabin. If you ask enough questions before you book the rental, you probably will not be frustrated during your stay.

TEST THE WATERS

We always try to test the waters before we jump into a long stay in a cabin. This allows us to try out a cabin for an overnight stay before we commit to spending a long weekend or an entire vacation in it. To do this, we often plan a long weekend that will find us in two or three cabins during that time. Friday night we will camp in one cabin. Saturday, we move to a new location and another cabin. Sunday, we're on the road again to yet another cabin. By doing this, we are able to scope out the features and benefits of multiple places without any long-term commitment.

The test-and-go methods we use have saved us from being disappointed on vacations and extended camping trips. Once we have compiled a list of good cabins, we can rest assured that our extended stays will be enjoyable.

THE BENEFITS OF CABIN CAMPING

The benefits of cabin camping are many. Let's look at some of the good points of spending time away from home in a cozy cabin.

Staying Dry

Cabins allow you to stay dry during the wettest of weather. Tents sometimes leak, especially tents without flys. Do you remember camping when you were a child and touching the roof of your tent during a rainstorm? Remember how the water came right through the tent and ran down your finger? Well, the roofs of cabins are not so sensitive, and you will not wake up floating on your air mattress.

Keeping Warm

Keeping warm in a tent, or even in some RVs, can be a problem on damp, cold days. Take a rainy day with cold camping quarters, and you have a miserable camping trip. This won't happen when you elect to camp in a cabin.

Security

Security is an issue that often comes to mind when adults think of taking their children camping. A thin, nylon barrier between your child and the elements doesn't make for a lot of security. Even a pop-up camper lacks the type of security some people need to feel comfortable. A cabin, however, offers all the security we have grown accustomed to in living inside four walls and under a sturdy roof.

Lighting

Lighting may not be one of the first things you think of when camping, but if you start out camping in a tent, you may soon notice the importance of good lighting. Children almost always enjoy having their parents read to them, and reading for long periods of time in dim lighting is not fun. Cabins, even ones without electricity (they offer gas lamps), usually provide good lighting for reading, cooking and general activities.

Food

Food storage and preparation are much easier in a cabin than in a tent. When you are cabin camping, you don't have to hang your food cache from the highest tree or wash your dishes with bottled water or in a stream. Most cabins are equipped with refrigerators that are much more efficient than ice chests, and the food won't get soggy.

Cooking over a campfire takes some practice, and not everyone enjoys the permeating smell of wood smoke blowing into their faces and clothes. Since cabins are generally equipped with modern cookstoves, the preparation of meals and baby formula is much easier than it is under the stars.

Sleeping

Sleeping in a nice comfortable bed has certain advantages over sleeping on damp, cold ground. Even with the best foam pads or air mattresses, it is hard to compare sleeping in a tent with sleeping in a regular bed.

Space to Move Around

Having space to move around inside your camping shelter is a big asset offered by cabins. Some RVs and tents are large enough to keep a family from going stir-crazy, but none of the RVs or tents can give you the freedom of movement possible in a cabin. This is a major advantage if the weather turns bad.

In general, cabin camping is a great way to get your whole family interested in the camping experience. Kids of all ages can enjoy spending time away from home in the comfort and security of a cabin, and nature can be right outside the front door.

WHERE CAN I FIND CAMPING CABINS?

Where can I find camping cabins? Many campgrounds that cater to tenters and RVers have some cabins available. There are also places where the entire complex is made up of cabins. Camping directories that will direct you to campgrounds with cabins are available at local bookstores, and most cabin-only facilities can also be found through advertisements in newspapers, outdoor magazines and phone directories. Local offices of the Chamber of Commerce can frequently provide you with brochures on various cabin-camping facilities.

If you have never tried camping in a cabin, you should. Of all the types of camping we do, cabin camping is one of our favorites.

Chapter Fifteen

CAMPING WITH AN RV

Camping with an RV allows you to rough it in comfort. There are many types of RVs available; they range from simple pop-up tent trailers to elaborate motorhomes. Your needs and budget considerations are the only constraints when seeking a suitable RV.

The process of evaluating the need for an RV can be confusing, and sorting through all of the possible options can get frustrating. Over the years we have done a lot of research on the various types of RVs, and we have used just about every type imaginable.

POP-UP CAMPERS

Pop-up campers are basically tents on wheels that provide comforts which are not feasible with regular tents. For example, pop-up campers can be equipped with furnaces, which is a real plus when camping in a cool climate with young children.

Many campers have an aversion to sleeping at ground level. For these campers, pop-ups provide an elevated shelter and peace of mind. This is especially important when camping with young children. (See photo p. 127.)

What other amenities will you get in a pop-up? Well, the list of options for these tent trailers is extensive. You can have a refrigerator, bathroom, cookstove, oven, fresh-water holding tanks, electricity, a hard-top, a soft-top, an awning and more.

Pop-Up Camper Advantages

Storage. Unless you have a van or a large truck rather than the family car, packing all the normal camping gear can be an adventure in itself, especially with kids. Pop-up trailers give you an edge in this department. There is plenty of room for stuffed animals, board games, dolls, footballs and other items of importance to your children.

Easy towing. Pop-ups are easy to tow, and many of them are light enough to be towed behind compact cars, and the lightweights

Soft-side pop-up camper

don't require expensive hitches or electric brakes. Since pop-ups fold down, they have little wind resistance when in tow. This makes for better gas mileage and less swaying on the road.

Electricity. Electricity is another advantage offered with tent trailers. If you are camping in a commercial campground, you can plug the cord from your trailer into an electrical hook-up. This gives you electricity for lights, and appliances, as well as televisions, VCRs, etc. If you don't have an electric hookup close by, you can use the on-board battery in the pop-up. Having electricity can make camping with kids much more enjoyable, especially on rainy days.

The Disadvantages of Pop-Ups

Pop-ups are trailers. Pop-ups are trailers, and towing any type of trailer can be annoying. However, for most people the many advantages of a pop-up over a tent outweigh the disadvantage of having to tow the RV.

Longevity. Properly cared for, a good pop-up will last many years without major expenses. However, without routine maintenance, pop-ups will not endure the test of time. For this reason, travel trailers are considered a better long-term investment.

Size. The size of pop-ups can be a disadvantage when compared to other RVs. While pop-ups provide plenty of room for sleeping, most don't allow a lot of room for moving around. You will find when you begin to spend time in an RV with your children that the more space you have, the more enjoyable the trip will be.

Some Questions

Are pop-up campers a good investment? In terms of a financial return on your money, no. However, pop-ups can provide years of camping enjoyment and offer advantages that are unobtainable with traditional tents. Are pop-ups a viable option for parents camping with kids? Yes, pop-ups offer more security from things that go bump in the night than tents, and they can provide additional comfort to campers. How much will a new tent trailer cost? Prices on pop-ups normally range from less than $3,500 on up to $8,000 or more, depending on size, features and brand name.

Should I buy a used pop-up? A used pop-up that has been well cared for can prove to be a wise purchase. Many people buy RVs and rarely use them. When buying these units, the savings can be substantial. However, be cautious in buying a trailer that is too old, as it may not be equipped with modern safety features and may require extensive work on frames, wiring, gas piping, water piping, floors, walls, ceilings, and other aspects of the construction. The winter months usually produce the best deals on used campers.

TRAVEL TRAILERS, MOTORHOMES AND TRUCK CAMPERS

When you begin to think of buying a travel trailer, motorhome, or a slide-in truck camper, you are thinking in terms of big bucks. All of these RVs are expensive. But, if you have the money and want maximum comfort while camping, these choices are the way to go.

If you slide a full-featured camper into the back of your pickup truck, you don't have to be concerned with the dangers and inconveniences of towing a trailer. There is also the advantage of not having much to do to set up camp when you arrive at the campsite with anxious children.

Travel trailers may be the most practical, cost-effective way to achieve maximum luxury at affordable prices. For less than $10,000 you can put your family into a fairly ritzy trailer. However, you may also have to invest in a tow vehicle.

Slide-In Truck Campers

A slide-in truck camper is a self-contained camper that slides into the bed of a pickup truck. Slide-in truck campers are an ideal means of shelter for some people. A full-size truck camper will easily tip the cash scales above the $10,000 mark. What do you get for your money? Plenty! Today's slide-in truck campers can be equipped with just about any option, though we've never seen one with a whirlpool tub. Some of the choices available to you include:

Awnings	Retractable steps
Exterior storage compartments	Porch lights
Roof vents	Sliding cab windows
Tripod mechanical jacks	Padded head knockers
Window shades	Range hoods
Exterior electrical outlets	Stereos
Four-burner ranges	Microwave ovens
Monitor panels	Ice boxes
Refrigerators	TV antennas, with rotors
Water heaters	Full bathrooms
Air-conditioning	Furnaces
Battery boxes	Gas bottles

Truck campers are great for individuals or couples, but they tend to be cramped when families occupy them. Due to their design, there is rarely much room for the kids to romp around in.

Motorhomes

Motorhomes (see photo p. 130) are beyond the financial reach of many campers. Small motorhomes are priced around $25,000, and midsize land yachts start at $35,000 and go up, way up. Unless you are independently wealthy or are planing a new lifestyle where you live in your new motorhome full time, you probably won't be able to justify the purchase.

The advantages of motorhomes. The advantages of motorhomes are many. You can drive until you find a place you like and stop for the night, without having to set anything up. If it rains, you

Motorhome

won't get wet and you never have to leave the inside of your mobile motel. When the kids get tired of riding, they can rest in comfort. However, we're firm believers in seat belts and don't think people should move around much or sleep while these vehicles are in motion.

The luxury available in motorhomes can rival the most prestigious homes. If you want maximum comfort and can afford it, motorhomes will give it to you.

The disadvantages of motorhomes. Big motorhomes are cumbersome in traffic, and they can be hard to park. Leaving your campsite for a run to the local store will be much more of a burden in a motorhome than it would be in a car or light truck. Upkeep and insurance can also be a distinct disadvantage in these high-priced toys.

Travel Trailers

Travel trailers (see photo p. 131) attract a lot of attention from comfort-oriented campers. These units provide varying levels of luxury at prices many campers can afford, even if they have to finance

Travel trailer

their purchase. Like all RVs, travel trailers have their ups and downs. Since these units are very popular, let's spend some time digging into the facts on their features and benefits.

Park and drop. Travel trailers offer the advantage of park-and-drop convenience. Once the trailer is parked, the tow vehicle can be disconnected and used for jaunts to the store or to explore the countryside. The advantage of being able to drive a conventional vehicle for your running around is a definite advantage.

No motor to deal with. Travel trailers have no motor to deal with. Since these units are trailers, they can log thousands of miles across country without concern of a major breakdown. While you will have to monitor the condition of your tow vehicle, the travel trailer can go on for years with minimal maintenance.

Cost advantages. Travel trailers have cost advantages over motorhomes. Trailers have starting prices of around $7,000 and like any RV with kitchen, sleeping and bathroom provisions, tax advantages are a possibility with your purchase.

Room to roam. Large travel trailers provide privacy and room to roam, even for families. While sleeping provisions will often ac-

Fifth-wheel travel trailer

commodate six to eight people, large travel trailers offer much more. You can buy trailers with bunk beds and master-bedroom suites. Having a bathroom with a tub or shower is no problem. Like motorhomes, travel trailers are available with a long list of options.

Fifth-Wheel Trailers

Fifth-wheel trailers (see photo above) are popular with serious roadrunners. Fifth-wheelers are not hooked to a standard hitch; they connect to a special type of hitch that mounts in the bed of a pickup truck or other suitable tow vehicle.

Serious RVers like fifth-wheel trailers because of their stability on the road. Having the trailer mounted over the axle of the tow vehicle makes for easier towing.

While fifth-wheelers are usually associated with big trucks, there are models made for midsize pickups. If you plan to spend a lot of time towing your new trailer, consider a fifth-wheeler.

IN CLOSING

In closing, I suggest that you shop extensively before you buy any RV. Take your children with you during your RV investigations. We have been amazed at what our five-year-old has noticed that we overlooked.

Since my first experience with a travel trailer, I have bought others. I have also bought tents and found them to be more convenient for my on-the-move, never-knowing-where-you-will-wind-up camping tactics. Before you lay out a lot of cash or sign on the dotted line for an expensive RV, give serious consideration to the pleasures of camping in a high-quality tent.

Chapter Sixteen

ORGANIZED CAMPGROUNDS

Organized campgrounds are a good place for new campers to get started. Many of these facilities offer extensive amenities, and help is never far away when you need it. When you are just learning to set up your tent or level out your RV, it's nice to know there is knowledgeable help close by.

Commercial campgrounds have something for everyone, and they range from semiprimitive to luxurious. Your children can enjoy the playgrounds, swimming pools and game rooms. You can relax around the fire ring or catch a few fish in one of the stocked ponds available at many campgrounds. If the dirty laundry is piling up, you can take it down to the coin-operated laundry often provided by campgrounds. When the itch for a hot shower hits you, a short walk should allow you to wash away your troubles. If you don't like the idea of finding a secluded spot to use your portable toilet, the clean bathrooms found at most campgrounds will be appreciated.

Camping in an organized campground can seem like a fancy vacation, or it can simulate the feel of a semiwilderness setting. How your stay at the campground goes will depend on the type of facility you choose. There are campgrounds with rivers running past them and campgrounds with stocked trout ponds; campgrounds with snowmobile trails, horseback riding and whirlpool spas, and many other amenities. You can choose the level of civilization you want. There are even campgrounds that offer babysitting services.

How much will a night at a campground cost? Costs vary as much as campground quality. You can find a tent site for the whole family for less than ten dollars a night, or you could spend thirty dollars a night. Prices are not hard to determine if you have a good campground directory.

CAMPGROUND DIRECTORIES
Campground directories can be found in most any bookstore. These thick books contain hundreds, possibly thousands, of listings for all

types of campgrounds. Using the directories is almost like mail-order shopping for a campsite. By scanning the pages of a good directory, you can learn a lot about a campground.

While we rarely make reservations for campsites (I find reservations too confining), we do use campground directories as guidebooks. We sit in the comfort of our living room with our daughter and conjure up all kinds of images of our next camping trip. Even when the plan is to rough it in primitive areas, we find directories helpful in gaining background information on the area and the sites available.

Campground directories don't list every campground, but they don't miss many. If you want to take a vacation to northern Maine, for example, flipping through the pages of a directory will tell you where campgrounds can be found, how much they charge, what amenities they offer, and how many choices are available. If your camping preference runs to deserts and canyons, you can find listings in the directories that will guide you to western campsites. Regardless of where you want to camp, campground directories are a valuable resource.

Maps. Most directories are broken down by states and provide maps of the areas. Generally, the states are listed in alphabetical order.

Prices. Directories list prices for various campgrounds. This makes shopping within a budget easy. You can see how much each campground charges for its minimum rate. If there are additional charges for multiple people or pets, the fees will be shown. If the campground charges for amenities, like hot showers, the directory will indicate the additional cost of these options. The prices reflect the difference in cost for a no-hookup site and a site with water or full hookups. You will also be told if the campground accepts credit cards and if so, what kind of cards they take.

Local attractions. Many local attractions are likely to be listed in campground directories. These are helpful in planning your event itinerary.

Annual events. Annual events is another category you will probably find in your directory. These listings give dates and details for routine events throughout the year, such as Fourth of July celebrations.

Site descriptions. Site descriptions are a big help in determining where you want to spend your time. Directories give you plenty of information on what to expect in terms of sites. For example, the directory listing might state that Bill's Lakeside Camps has twenty sites with full hookups, seventeen sites with water and electric hookups, forty tent sites with no hookups, and six cabins. The listing might go on to describe how many of the sites are wooded, open, or waterfront.

Dates of operation. The dates of operation will be listed for all campgrounds. If the camps open on Memorial Day and close after Labor Day, the directory will tell you.

Activities. A list of activities offered by each campground will be found in your directory. These activities could include: fishing, swimming, tennis, basketball, horseshoes, playgrounds, hiking, snowmobiling, badminton, volleyball, coin-operated arcade games, libraries, horseback riding, trapshooting, skeet shooting, and so on. Workout rooms, spas, billiard rooms, and recreational halls may also be listed.

Directions, phone numbers and addresses. Directions to the campgrounds, phone numbers and addresses will be found in campground directories. You can easily inquire for more details on the facilities, and the directions are usually good enough to get you to the sites, without additional instructions from the campground operators.

Display ads. Display ads, found throughout the directories, tell you more about the various campgrounds. Unlike the listings, these ads are paid for by the campgrounds and are intended to interest you in their facilities. By reading the display ads and the directory listings, you can get to know a lot about the many different campgrounds.

Read Between the Lines

You have to read between the lines to find the best facilities. There is plenty of information supplied by campground directories, but to make the most of it, you have to learn how to interpret the details. You should study the listings closely and pick up on the little pointers that might go unnoticed in a quick scan. Let me give you an example of what I'm talking about.

When we read a directory listing, we see much more that just the words on the page. When we look at the display ads for various campgrounds, we look for the tone taken in the ads. This type of dissection allows us to draw some conclusions as to the type of campground we are really reading about.

When we go camping in commercial campgrounds, we like to have access to certain amenities, but we don't want to be surrounded by an army of howling kids and drunken campers. On the other hand, since we have a five-year-old, we enjoy having some kids available for her to play with, and we don't want to be the only party in the campground with an excitable and often audible child.

Finding a campground that provides swimming and a playground, while maintaining a secluded atmosphere, can be a challenge. However, our success rate for reading between the lines of campground directories is a good one. Let's get specific on what you should look for.

Group tenting sites. If you see a listing that describes group tenting sites, you can normally be sure you are not headed into a campground that offers seclusion. This is an obvious red flag for families like ours. This type of camping provides cheap sleep, but no privacy.

There are, however exceptions to this line of thinking. Some campgrounds have group tenting sites to accommodate groups of friends that are camping together. This way, when a snowmobile club wants to camp together, they have their own private area. This type of approach separates large groups from individual campers and actually provides better privacy for everyone.

Large, wooded sites. When I see a listing that talks about large, wooded sites, my ears perk up. There is a real possibility of some solitude in campgrounds with these sites.

Flush toilets. I've got nothing against flush toilets, but I see this aspect of a listing to mean a modern, commercial campground. If we're looking for a simulated wilderness adventure, we might pass over these listings.

Pit toilets. A listing that contains pit toilets indicates either a wilderness environment or a cheap campground.

Hot showers. A campground that has hot showers will usually have electricity, but not always. Remote camps, like some of those found in Maine, use LP gas to heat water for their showers. It is also likely that these campgrounds cater to long-term campers, generally RVers. This type of listing isn't going to stop us from investigating further, but we quickly tend to draw a mental picture of motor-homes and trailers.

Laundry facilities. Finding laundry facilities in a directory listing is another indication of a campground looking for long-term guests, though some campground owners told us that laundry facilities are used more by one-nighters than long-term campers. However, you are probably going to find a high ratio of high-dollar RVs. You might also expect to find a more mature group of people in these camps.

Tennis courts. Tennis courts could mean the campground is centered around couples. Tennis courts shouldn't be an immediate turnoff if you are looking for rustic conditions, but they do raise the level of investigation needed to determine campground conditions.

Horseshoe pits. Horseshoe pits might mean running into some of the good old boys. I enjoy playing horseshoes, but the constant clanging of metal on metal might be disruptive to some campers. Adult horseshoes are metal, and they are heavy. It is not uncommon for horseshoes to go flipping, bouncing and rolling for some dis-tance from their intended target. This can create a safety risk for small children, so make sure your youngsters don't get too close to the pits when a game is being played.

Ponds, lakes and rivers. Ponds, lakes and rivers are generally considered assets for a campground. However, if your children are young, these assets may turn into liabilities. The risk of having a child fall into the water and drown may worry you so much that you will not enjoy your stay.

Playgrounds. Campgrounds that have playgrounds are expect-ing to accommodate young children. If a campground doesn't have a playground, it may cater to an older group.

Basketball courts. Basketball courts will usually be occupied by teenagers and young adults. This type of amenity can be a negative factor if your kids are young.

Swimming pools. Swimming pools are sought after by all age groups. When a campground has invested in a pool, it stands to reason that the campsites may be a cut above the rest.

Pets. Pets can be a sensitive issue when camping. While your

A happy fishing day

children may not want to leave home without them, campground operators may not let you in with them. Again, campground directories can help you. Most listings in directories will tell you if the campground allows pets.

THE BENEFITS

The benefits of organized campgrounds are numerous. Your children will find many activities to keep them busy and interested. As a parent, you can benefit from the freedom offered by these semiprotected environments. Unlike the remote wilderness, organized campgrounds provide a partial barrier between your kids and unknown dangers.

Convenience is also a big factor in these facilities. It can be nice to walk over to the in-camp store or stroll over to the public phone. These are features you won't find in outback camps.

Structured campgrounds are not the answer for all campers, but they do offer a lot of advantages for family camping. They also make an excellent training ground for novice campers. Before you leave the pavement behind for the dusty trails of the wild country, give yourself the opportunity to refine your camping skills in an organized campground.

Chapter Seventeen

BASIC TIPS FOR NOVICE CAMPERS

Campsite safety is instrumental to happy camping. Nobody is going to enjoy camping trips where they, or their loved ones, are injured. Many of the potential dangers around camp are not monumental, but they can, nevertheless, ruin an otherwise great outing.

Unlike most of the book, this chapter is going to give you many suggestions in quick succession. This machine-gun style of text will allow you to pick and choose the suggestions that are most applicable to you.

SAFETY SUGGESTIONS

Setting Up Camp

- Never pitch a tent in the mountains where there is evidence of a gully or old waterways. What is a gully or dried-up streambed when you go to sleep could be a raging river when you awake. As their name implies, flash floods happen quickly. A quick look at the lay of the land will tell you if you are in the path of a potential flash flood.

- Widow Maker is the name given to suspended tree branches and trees with dead tops. If the wind picks up, this dead wood can come crashing down, inflicting serious injuries. Before you pitch camp, always look up, and never camp under trees that may drop on you.

- Don't set your camp up in the middle of a game trail. There is nothing worse than having a herd of deer come crashing through your camp in the middle of the night. If there is a defined path in the leaves or grass, avoid making camp near it.

- If you are camping during hunting season, make your camp and yourself visible to hunters.

- Don't set up camp on shaky ground. Banks and cliffs can be eroded to a point where they might give way at any time.

• Don't make camp where rock outcroppings are positioned above you. You never know when the rocks might start rolling in your direction.

• Avoid tent stakes that will impale falling campers.

• Avoid setting tent-support strings in a way to cause tripping.

• Keep the screens to your tent closed at all times. You don't want snakes, spiders and other uninvited guests taking up residency in your home away from home.

• Before you pitch your tent, clear the ground in the tent site. Setting up camp on top of a yellow-jacket nest is no fun, and neither is sleeping over an animal or snake den. Check under the natural ground cover to be sure your tent will only be pressing against natural earth.

Equipment Safety

• Don't leave axes, mauls, saws, knives, and the like lying around. These sharp tools can spell disaster around kids and unco-ordinated campers. If your bladed instruments don't have sheaths, bury the blades in dead wood or make other provisions to keep people from being cut or impaled.

• If you take a gun to camp, make sure it is stored safely. Firearm accidents are numerous, but can be easily prevented. Though an unloaded gun is of little value in a time of need, a loaded gun left carelessly about provides potential for irreparable damage or loss. If you feel the need for a gun to protect your children, you should probably relocate to a safer campsite. What starts out as protection could wind up as a heartache.

Fire Safety

• Don't get too close to your campfire. Some types of clothing are very flammable. A quick change in the direction of the wind can have your clothes on fire before you know it. If this happens, drop to the ground and roll over and over, to smother the fire.

• Don't leave your campfire burning unattended. When you are done with the fire, extinguish it, thoroughly.

• Never throw flammable liquids on a smoldering fire to get it going; you may get more fire than you bargained for. If necessary, put the fire out completely, and start over.

• *Never* dispose of spent LP-gas cylinders in the campfire.

• Sitting by the fire with your boots propped up on the rock fireplace is relaxing, but it can also melt the soles off of your boots.

• If you dry your clothes by the campfire, be careful of putting them on too quickly after drying them. Brass buttons, snaps and zippers can get very hot. Jumping into your jeans too quickly after drying them can result in some embarrassing burns.

• Don't throw used food cans into the fire. Burning them might attract animals.

• Soybean oil is highly flammable. If you like eating sardines or fish steaks that come packed in soybean oil, be advised that the oil produces a quick flare-up if thrown in the fire.

• Don't burn wood that is surrounded by poison ivy. The smoke from the poison ivy could trigger skin irritations and respiratory problems.

• Don't throw leaves and loose materials, like paper, into a burning fire. These light objects are likely to catch fire and be blown into the air, carrying fire into unwanted areas.

• Never take a gas-fired lantern, stove or heater into a tent. The heat from these items could set the tent on fire; also, the depletion of oxygen, due to its use by the equipment, might cause asphyxiation.

• Aerosol cans and batteries thrown into a fire may explode.

• Wet rocks placed in or around a hot fire can explode.

• Dirt will serve as a fine natural fire extinguisher as it smothers a flame.

Eating and Drinking

• Don't eat unidentified forest foods.

• Purify all wild water before drinking it. Even in the most remote wilderness, you never know what died in the water a few hundred yards upstream.

• Before eating the fish you catch, make sure the water is not polluted to a point where the fish may be hazardous to your health.

• Keep empty food containers and soiled paper plates in a bag that is suspended from a high tree limb.

- Hang your food cache high in a tree, away from your tent.
- Don't attempt to feed or handle wild animals.
- Animals in wild areas that don't show fear of your presence may be infected with rabies. If an animal acts tame, avoid it and move out of the area quickly.
- Never eat in your tent or leave food in your tent.
- Wash dishes a safe distance from camp. If you don't, any scrapings you leave behind could be an engraved invitation for night visits from a variety of wild animals.

General Safety
- Don't let your kids play too close to streams, rivers, lakes and ponds. Even the most shallow water can become a death trap when a person slips and is knocked unconscious.
- Unless you are very experienced, never walk on, camp on, or investigate ice-covered water. Even after testing ice with an auger, there is no guarantee the thickness is uniform. A fall into ice-covered water is likely to be fatal.
- Teach your kids to respect campstoves, fishhooks and other common camp hazards.
- Always have a first-aid kit in camp, and know how to use it.
- If you must smoke, don't smoke in your tent, and be careful when discarding the remains of your lighted tobacco product.
- Develop emergency plans. For example, instruct your children what to do and how to get out if the RV catches on fire.
- If you are going into the wilderness, never take helpless children on the journey when you are the only attending adult. What would your child do if you were disabled suddenly? A six-year-old is not going to be able to drive out of the woods for help. You will be endangering not only your own life, but the lives of those with you.
- If you are a single parent and want to experience backcountry camping, use the buddy system. Find another adult, perhaps another single parent, to join you and your child on the adventure. Not only is this a safe solution, it can be more enjoyable for you and your child.
- Don't wander through the wilderness in the dark; you never know what you might bump into.

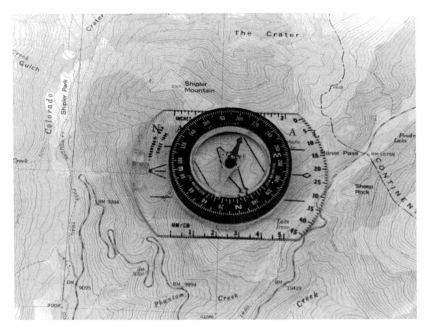

Compass and topographical map

- Use topographical maps to aid in locating and avoiding old mining pits and shafts.
- Learn first-aid techniques.
- Acquire a compass and a topographical map of the area you will be visiting, and learn how to use them.
- Study animal behavior so that you will understand animals rather than fear them.
- Tell friends or family where you will be camping and when you expect to return. If something serious happens to you, at least someone will know to start looking for you and where to begin the search.
- Provide every camper with a survival kit and instructions on how to use it.
- Keep a close eye on your kids, even big ones; it is easy to get lost only a few hundred yards from camp.

RV Safety

- If you are camping in an RV, check your LP-gas tubing before using your appliances. A bumpy ride can loosen the connections on the gas tubing and cause leaks. These leaks can be deadly. To check for leaks, turn on the gas and rub soapy water on all connections. If the water bubbles, you've got a leak.

• When you park your RV, stabilize it with jacks, and place chocks under the tires to prevent it from rolling away.

• Keep a spare set of car keys hidden out. You don't want to lock your only set of keys in your car when you are miles from the nearest locksmith.

• Don't store flammable liquids in your tent, RV, or near any source of flame or high heat.

• If you are car-camping, take along a fire extinguisher. Backpackers cannot justify the extra weight, but if you are hauling your gear by vehicle, you have no excuse for not having at least one fire extinguisher on hand. When you purchase your fire extinguisher, check to see what types of fires it is effective on. Not all fire extinguishers are designed to work with the same types of fire.

• If you are camping in an RV, check electrical wires and connections carefully.

This concise list of suggestions will help you avoid many of the blunders made by first-time campers. Before you go afield, refer to this chapter and make sure you have committed the rules of safe camping to memory.

Chapter Eighteen

FIRST-AID AND SURVIVAL SUGGESTIONS

This chapter lists some first-aid tips and common remedies. However, we are not medical doctors: The information given here is for illustrative purposes only and is not how-to advice. Never administer medicine or complicated medical assistance unless you are properly trained.

Before we go on, let us address the issue of teaching your kids about first-aid procedures and injuries in general. As a parent, it is your job to provide education for your children. Part of this job should include an education in first aid and emergency conditions.

A child who knows first-aid may save your life. But, there is more to this issue than bandaging a cut or treating a sting from a bee.

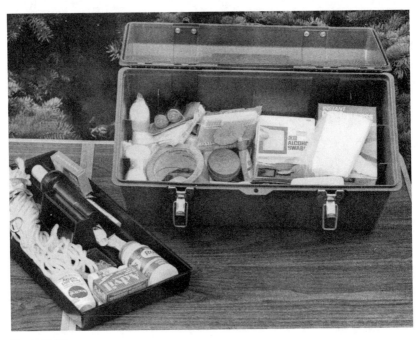

First-aid kit

Children love their parents and could react strongly if a parent is injured suddenly. A child may go into shock, panic, or be just plain scared.

By teaching children how to react in the case of an emergency, you can reduce the mental stress your child will experience. Further, you prepare the child to make rational decisions under stress. This training can be very important if you or your child becomes injured or ill.

SERIOUS MEDICAL EMERGENCIES

When I worked in law enforcement and served in rescue services there were three types of emergencies that were reason to run the emergency vehicle full out: bleeding, breathing and poisoning. A lost minute in reacting to these emergencies could be fatal for the victim.

If you are faced with these types of emergencies in the wilderness, you may not have time to get the suffering person to a hospital. It is under these conditions that you will be thankful for every minute you spent in a professionally instructed first-aid class.

Due to the serious nature of these big-three emergencies, and the side effects that can happen if the wrong steps are taken, I am going to give you but one piece of advice: attend a certified first-aid class before putting yourself and your family into remote wilderness situations. Now, let's look at some of the other types of medical concerns you may be confronted with.

OTHER INJURIES AND MEDICAL CONCERNS

Minor bleeding can usually be controlled by applying and maintaining pressure on the wound. While a strip of clothing can act as a bandage in an emergency, sterile gauze is a better choice.

A simple sewing kit can be used to close large wounds. Tape can also be used to hold a gaping wound together. However, these are only temporary solutions, and expert medical help should be sought immediately following first-aid procedures.

Infections can develop from seemingly simple wounds. By treating wounds with disinfectants, there is less risk of future complications.

Don't move a person who has taken a fall. Moving the individual could result in permanent damage. Consult with the victim and determine what hurts. Have the person slowly attempt to use various body parts. A sudden movement, such as picking your child up, could have disastrous effects. There is, however, one exception to this rule. If the injured victim is in danger from additional, serious injury, movement may be necessary. This type of condition might apply to relocating a person from a fire or other impending disaster.

Broken bones are an injury that may be experienced in the woods. If you suspect a bone is broken, immobilize the area around the bone. Don't attempt to straighten the limb or set the bone; simply immobilize it. Once the immobilization is complete, transport the victim to professional medical care.

Shock

A person can go into shock from receiving an injury or from observing someone else being injured. For example, compound fractures are ugly, and a child seeing a parent suffer this type of injury could go into shock.

Symptoms of shock may be weakness, a loss of color, erratic breathing, dizziness, shaking, nausea, and cold or clammy-feeling skin. Shock can occur well after the incident of injury has occurred.

When shock is suspected, calm the victim. Make the victim comfortable and control body temperature with appropriate means, such as wrapping the body in a blanket or sleeping bag. A prone position is usually recommended for shock victims. Once the individual is stabilized, seek medical evaluation.

Burns and Blisters

Burns are rated in degrees. There are first-degree, second-degree, and third-degree burns. Minor burns can be treated with a dip in cool water or ice, followed by the application of lotions designed to help minor burns. However, serious burns need fast medical attention. If the skin is blistered or open, don't apply bandages to the area.

Blisters are likely when campers are wearing new footwear or using their hands for cutting wood and similar duties that they are not accustomed to. Wearing gloves on the hands and boots that fit properly are the best ways to avoid blisters. However, if blisters begin to occur, early treatment will minimize the discomfort. An adhesive bandage placed over newly forming blisters can retard the blistering.

Blisters that grow and break open can turn serious. These are open wounds, and infection can move in. Treat broken blisters as you would an open wound. Clean the wound and apply a disinfectant. Then, cover the wound with a non-clinging bandage.

Eye Injuries

Eye contamination may occur while camping. If a victim splashes a foreign liquid in an eye, flush the eye with water immediately. Bathe the eye for ten minutes with a gentle stream of the cleanest water available. Be careful not to contaminate the other eye while flushing the affected eye. After the flushing of the eye is complete, swab the outside areas surrounding the eye, and place a patch over the eye.

If a foreign object, like a piece of tree bark, gets in the eye, be careful. Movement of the eyeball could cause the foreign particle to scratch the eye or do other damage. If properly trained, you will know how to remove loose foreign objects from the eye. However, inexperienced attempts at removing objects from an eye can result in permanent damage.

In all cases, after first aid is administered, proceed immediately to professional medical help.

Hypothermia

Hypothermia can strike even in what seems to be warm weather. If a person, especially a child, falls into or plays in cold water, hypothermia can result quickly. Even perspiring profusely can be enough to bring on hypothermia.

Some signs of hypothermia include: feeling cold, having a low body temperature, chattering teeth, shivering, a loss of motor skills, trouble walking and talking, slow pulse and respiration, confusion, and even unconsciousness. Hypothermia is a serious threat.

If hypothermia is suspected, treat the victim quickly. Get the person warm. If the condition is mild, administer warm food or liquids, but be alert to possible choking. If the situation has elevated to more severe hypothermia, warm the body and discourage unnecessary movement. One way to warm the person in a camping situation is to crawl into a sleeping bag with the individual. Your body heat and the heat retention of the sleeping bag will help to warm the victim more quickly.

Hypothermia and frostbite are both serious concerns. When these conditions exist, seek medical help quickly.

Stings and Bites

Bee stings can be fatal. If a person is allergic to the bites and stings of various creatures, a minor discomfort can become life threatening. If traveling with companions who have allergic reactions to bites and stings, never leave home without their medication.

For more normal run-ins with stings and bites, baking soda and water will provide some relief. There are also commercial ointments and such that can be used to treat minor stings and bites.

Nosebleeds

Some people have nosebleeds for no apparent reason. Simple nosebleeds can be stopped by applying pressure to the nose for about five minutes. Packing the nostril with cotton before applying pressure is also sometimes recommended. If the bleeding doesn't stop within ten to fifteen minutes, head for the hospital, while maintaining the packing and pressure.

Heat-Related Problems

Heat exhaustion is caused by a lack of body fluids and salt. This condition can arise while being active in hot weather. Possible signs of heat exhaustion might include: a loss of color, nausea, a fast pulse, headache and dizziness.

Treating minor heat exhaustion could be as simple as removing clothing and cooling the body with water or ice. Sipping water will be helpful, but avoid gulping. Too much liquid, too fast, can complicate matters. In the process of treating heat exhaustion, be careful not to set the stage for an onset of hypothermia.

Heatstroke is more serious than heat exhaustion, and heat cramps can develop under conditions associated with both heat exhaustion and heatstroke. When cramping occurs, the body needs electrolytes. With heatstroke, victims need to be cooled and transported for prompt medical attention.

Various Aches and Pains

Toothaches can ruin a camping trip. Minor tooth and gum pain can be relieved with over-the-counter numbing agents.

Headaches can usually be conquered with standard, over-the-counter remedies.

Sprained ankles and similar conditions are painful. These conditions mimic a broken bone and should be treated as such. Immobilize the limb and transport the person for medical evaluation.

Sunburn can and should be avoided. However, when skin is burned by the sun's rays, treat it gently. A soothing lotion will ease discomfort. If the skin blisters, avoid clinging clothes and attempt to keep the blisters from breaking.

Barbed fishhooks can create panic in the camp. If these ornery objects become embedded in the skin, apply ice to the wound and head for a doctor. The hook will probably be pushed through the skin, so that the barb can be cut off and the remainder of the hook can be removed. This procedure should be done by skilled medical personnel. When we take Afton fishing, we use a pair of pliers to squeeze in the barb on her hook. She is still able to catch fish, but if she should hook herself, or one of us—as she has done occasionally—the hook is easy to remove.

Ticks

Ticks can be more than annoying; they can carry serious diseases. If a tick has embedded itself in the skin, don't try to pull it loose; the head may break off, remaining in the skin and causing problems. Fingernail polish remover applied to the tick will sometimes make it turn loose. Brief exposure to a small flame, like a match or cigarette lighter, may make the tick give up its grip. Tweezers can be used to remove ticks, but make sure you get all of the tick out of the wound.

After removing the tick, pay attention to possible side effects. If a rash develops, headaches or muscle aches ensue, or unusual fatigue is encountered, consult a physician.

As I said earlier, these tips are merely examples of how complications might be treated, they are not official recommendations or advice. Gain your first-aid knowledge from qualified instructors.

Bedtime, Veni Montresor: Harper & Row, Publishers, Inc.

Bedtime for Frances, Russell Hoban: Harper & Row, Publishers, Inc.

Can't You Sleep, Little Bear?, Martin Waddell: Candlewick Press

A Child's Garden of Verses, Robert Louis Stevenson, with illustrations by Jessie Wilcox Smith

A Child's Goodnight Book, Margaret Wise Brown: A & W Publishers, Inc.

Dorothy's Dream, Kady MacDonald Denton: Thames & Hudson, Publishers

Dr. Seuss's Sleep Book, Dr. Seuss: Random House, Inc.

5-Minute Bunny Tales For Bedtime, S. Sheringham & J. Stimson: Derrydale Publishers

Franklin in the Dark, Paulette Bourgeois: Kids Can Press, Ltd.

Giant Treasury of Brer Rabbit, Harry Tountree & Renee Bull: Derrydale Publishers

Goodnight Moon, Margaret Wise Brown: Harper & Row, Publishers, Inc.

I Can Choose My Bedtime Story, edited by Mary Parsley: Grosset & Dunlap

Just Listen, Winifred Morris: Atheneum Publishers

Mooncake, Frank Asch: Simon & Schuster, Inc.

Moon Song, Mildred Plew Meigs: William Morrow & Company, Inc.

Night Noises and Other Mole and Troll Stories, Tony Johnston: G.P. Putnam's Sons

The Rainbabies, Laura Krauss Melmed & Jim Lamarche: William Morrow & Company, Inc.

Read To Me, Grandma, edited by Glorya Hale with illustrations by Jesse Wilcox Smith

The Snowdrop, Hans Christian Anderson with illustrations by Tizianna Gitoni

The Summer Night, Charlotte Zolotow: Harper & Row, Publishers, Inc.

Two Tiny Mice, Alan Baker, Penguin Books, USA Inc.

Where the Wild Things Are, Maurice Sendak: Harper & Row, Publishers, Inc.

APPENDIX B
FEDERAL RESOURCE INFORMATION

BUREAU OF LAND MANAGEMENT DIVISIONS
Bureau of Land Management
Office of Information
Department of the Interior
Washington, D.C. 20240

State Listings:
Arizona
2400 Valley Bank Center
Phoenix, Arizona 85073

California
Federal Office Building
2800 Cottage Way
Sacramento, California 95825

Colorado
2000 Arapahoe St.
Denver, Colorado 80205

Idaho
Box 042
Boise, Idaho 83724

Montana
Box 30157
Billings, Montana 59107

Nevada
Box 12000
Reno, Nevada 89520

New Mexico
Box 1449
Santa Fe, New Mexico 87501

Oregon
Box 2965
Portland, Oregon 97208

Utah
University Club Building
136 East South Temple
Salt Lake City, Utah 84111

Washington
Box 2965
Portland, Oregon 97208

Wyoming
Box 1828
Cheyenne, Wyoming 82001

NATIONAL PARK SERVICES
National Park Service
Department of the Interior
Washington, D.C. 20240

Regional Listings:
Alaska Region
540 West Fifth Ave.
Anchorage, Alaska 99501

Mid-Atlantic Region
143 South Third St.
Philadelphia, Pennsylvania 19106

Midwest Region
1709 Jackson St.
Omaha, Nebraska 68102

North Atlantic Region
15 State St.
Boston, Massachusetts 02109

Pacific Northwest Region
1920 Westin Building
2001 Sixth Ave.
Seattle, Washington 98121

Rocky Mountain Region
Box 25287
Denver, Colorado 80225

Southeast Region
75 Spring St. S.W.
Atlanta, Georgia 30303

Southwest Region
Box 728
Santa Fe, New Mexico 87501

Western Region
Box 36063
San Francisco, California 94102

FOREST SERVICES
U.S. Forest Service
Box 2417
Department of Agriculture
Washington, D.C. 20013

Regional Listings:
Alaska Region
Box 1628
Juneau, Alaska 99802

California Region
630 Sansome Street
San Francisco, California 94111

Eastern Region
633 West Wisconsin Ave.
Milwaukee, Wisconsin 53203

Intermountain Region
324 25th St.
Ogden, Utah 84401

Northern Region
Federal Building
Missoula, Montana 59807

Pacific Northwest Region
Box 3623
Portland, Oregon 97208

Rocky Mountain Region
Box 25217
Denver, Colorado 80225

Southern Region
1720 Peachtree Road, N.W.
Atlanta, Georgia 30309

INDEX

wearing hats, 78-79
wearing shoes, 78
Satellites, looking for, 100
Saws, 118-119
Scrapbooks, nature, 74-75
Shadow bunnies, making, 99
Shoes, 78
Shovels, 117-118
Sleep, ensuring good, 101-104
  controlling the temperature, 101-102
  dealing with animal visitors, 103
  dealing with noise, 102-103
  making your child comfortable, 101
  using night lights, 101
Sleeping, bags, 106-107
  designer, 106-107
  mummy, 107
  rectangular, 107
Sleeping, foundations, 107-108
  air mattresses, 108
  cots, 108
  foam pads, 108
Snow, sculpting, 74
Songs, travel, 45-46
Specimen, nature, collecting, 82
Star, gazing, 100
Stories, making up, 46
Stoves
  gasoline, 109-110
  liquid-fuel, 109-110
  propane, 109
Streams
  as a source of fire building materials, 87
  exploring, 70
Sundials, making, 80-81

T

Tables
  folding, 114

picnic, 114
roll-up, 114
seating, 114
Tents, 52, 67
  cabin, 105
  dome, 105
  modified-dome, 106
  poles, 53
  setting up, 14, 53-54
  umbrella, 53
Thunder, explaining, 64-65
Ticks
  dealing with, 151
  protective clothing, 21
  protective products, 21
Tinder, finding, for fires, 86
Toilet facilities
  bucket-style, 113
  privacy stall, 114
  simple, 112-113
  top-of-the-line, 113
  waste disposal, 117
Tools
  axes, hatchets and mauls, 118
  knives, 117
  saws, 118-119
  shovels, 117-118
Tools, for calming children's fears
  audio tapes, 10
  creature repellents, 20
  flashlights, 19
  library, 10
  videos, 10
Toys
  glow-in-the-dark, 101
  packing, 55
Trailers, fifth-wheel, 132
Trailers, travel, 52, 128-132
  features, 131-132
Traveling

More Great Books in The Parent's Guide Series!

Your influence as a coach or teacher can give children (both yours and others) the greatest gifts of all: strong self-confidence and high self-esteem. *The Parent's Guide* series has a dozen books full of helpful illustrations and step-by-step guides on how to nurture and encourage children as they strive for success in sports and the arts. Plus, the friendly, familiar tone of each book will help both you and the child have fun as you learn.

The Parent's Guide to Coaching Physically Challenged Children —
#70255/$12.95/144 pages/paperback

The Parent's Guide to Teaching Self-Defense —
#70254/$12.95/144 pages/paperback

The Parent's Guide to Coaching Baseball —
#70076/$7.95/128 pages/paperback

The Parent's Guide to Coaching Basketball —
#70077/$8.95/136 pages/paperback

The Parent's Guide to Coaching Football —
#70078/$8.95/144 pages/paperback

The Parent's Guide to Coaching Hockey —
#70216/$8.95/176 pages/paperback

The Parent's Guide to Coaching Soccer —
#70079/$8.95/136 pages/paperback

The Parent's Guide to Coaching Tennis —
#70080/$7.95/144 pages/paperback

The Parent's Guide to Coaching Skiing —
#70217/$8.95/144 pages/paperback

The Parent's Guide to Teaching Music —
#70082/$7.95/136 pages/paperback

The Parent's Guide to Band and Orchestra —
#70075/$7.95/136 pages/paperback

The Parent's Guide to Teaching Art:
How to Encourage Your Child's Artistic Talent and Ability —
#70081/$11.95/184 pages/paperback

Dozens of Great Ideas to Help You Get the Most Out of Life!

Raising Happy Kids on a Reasonable Budget — As seen on Oprah Winfrey! This one-of-a-kind guide is packed with dollar stretching techniques and budgeting tips you need to raise happy and healthy kids — whether you have one child or ten! *#70184/$10.95/144 pages/paperback*

Clutter's Last Stand — You're in clutter denial. You think you're perfectly organized, yet closets and drawers bulge around you. You'll get rid of clutter, in every aspect of your life, with this delightful, humorous guide full of practical advice. *#01122/$10.95/280 pages/paperback*

The Organization Map — You WILL defeat clutter and disorganization. This clear, effective, and encouraging guide is chock full of tips and advice for time-management, practical storage solutions, and more! *#70224/$12.95/208pages/paperback*

Confessions of an Organized Homemaker — You'll find hundreds of tips and ideas for organizing your household in this totally revised and updated edition. Discover motivation builders, consumer product information, and more! *#70240/$10.95/224 pages/paperback*

Slow Down and Get More Done — Discover precisely the right pace for your life by gaining control of worry, making possibilities instead of plans, and learning the value of doing "nothing." *#70183/$11.95/192 pages/paperback*

You Can Find More Time for Yourself Every Day — Professionals, working mothers, college students — if you're in a hurry, you need this time-saving guide! Quizzes, tests, and charts will show you how to make the most of your minutes! *#70258/$12.99/208 pages/paperback*

Streamlining Your Life — Finally, you'll get practical solutions to life's pesky problems and a 5-point plan to take care of tedious tasks. *#10238/$11.95/142 pages/paperback*

- rice in shaker
- radio
- wash basin
- coffee cups
- games for kids
- coloring books / crayons
- cards
- electrical covers
- bucket
- scrubby pad for general cleaning
- 409
- measuring cup